NIGHT COMES DOWN

by Bob Short

Published by Earth Island Books

Pickforde Lodge

Pickforde Lane

Ticehurst

East Sussex

TN5 7BN

www.earthislandbooks.com

Published by Earth Island Books 2025

ISBN 9781916864801 paperback

ISBN 9781916864818 ebook

Printed and bound by Solopress, Southend

IF NOTHING IS TRUE
IS EVERYTHING PERMITTED?

Foreword

"In Universities, they would talk about Punk in terms of a musical movement or an art movement. We were the more unpleasant reality. Whilst some played at dress ups, being a punk rocker in the squats of London was to leave civilization and enter a world of sub-Dickensian squalor. We entered the gates of the Kingdom of Abaddon and cold iron swung closed behind us." (quote from the book)

I first met Bob Short when we were both squatting in the fruit and veg warehouses opposite Covent Garden tube station in a complex that stretched around James Street and Long Acre. The multi-building edifice was going through a slow process of eviction, and many occupants had already moved on to a squatted fire station near Old Street.

Bob was suddenly living there one day in one of the rooms, along with Brett, Dave and Gordon. It was not clear where they had come from but such questions were rarely asked. We're here because we're here. I had moved in there one day through being taken to the place after a gig at the nearby Rock Garden, and never went back to my squatted pub off Ladbroke Grove.

We squatted strange buildings in those days, because we lived in strange days. Spring 1979 in London was a time of post-war dereliction and bomb-damage, post-hippy consolidation of Alternative London, post-Pistols punk, violence against punks, poverty, fascism, the arrival of Crass and Anarcho-Punk, squatting, and for people like Bob and myself, finding ourselves among the ruins.

I was a writer at that time, Bob remembers the inspiration he got from seeing me sitting on the floor, tapping away at a typewriter surrounded by James Street debris, whilst Bob had come to London to form a band. Bob did form a band, Blood & Roses, but he has also sat amongst his own mental and physical debris to tap out this incredible memoir.

Tracing his route to Spring 1979 Covent Garden through a trail of filth in Australia, growing up there as a stranger in a strange land, and from Oz through his journey as a London punk squatter that neither shies away from or glamorises the absolute squalor experienced. There are drugs, thugs, bugs, death, diseases and the diabolical all laid bare, till the end of Blood & Roses in 1985 when Bob declares, "I was rather keen on sleeping for a thousand years."

Blood & Roses have been written about a lot in my website Kill Your Pet Puppy, and for the website Bob himself has written about the Puppy fanzine plus other great pieces snatched from his compendious memory. Bob is a great writer, he asked me to write something for his book, "something that says you are a great writer, because you are."

To write writerly then, Bob spreads his world of the wretched out before you like a banquet from the bin, a naked lunch to be relished, "as a moment when everyone sees what is on the end of every fork," (thank you William Burroughs). Bob's work is an extraordinary feast, but wash your hands before and after reading, sometimes you may also feel like washing your eyes. Often you may feel like washing your eyes.

Tony Drayton, March 2025

(Tony Drayton, founder and editor of punk fanzine Ripped & Torn issues 1-17, founder and editor of punk fanzine Kill Your Pet Puppy issues 1-6, music journalist and cultural historian).

Introduction

When you are born, everyone looks down into your crib and imagines a bright future despite all evidence to the contrary. Sooner or later, Night comes down.

I have heard the chimes at midnight. Hell, I've dropped the pills and stayed awake to hear them chime again. You could call this my story but it is really just a story much like those of a thousand others. It's just many of those others didn't get to write their stories down. This is a story full of ghosts.

Many people's lives and stories are treated as proof that they are imbeciles or lunatics. When you're strange, faces come out of the rain to take the piss out of you. We were punk rockers; a minority made of our own dissent.

We became the fodder for bad comedians in search of a joke to make them feel relevant again; those sad old men with spiky haired wigs and fake safety pins. Mother-in-Law gags weren't cutting it anymore.

The old must mock the young and the new. The straights must mock variation because, after all, they are the weirdest fuckers in the world. If you don't fit in either by some trick of birth, accident or design, there will be consequences.

I can't promise you the whole truth and nothing but the truth because a lot of the time we all just sit on our arses doing sweet fuck all. They say war is months of boredom, interspaced with moments of terror.

I've tried to skip the boring bits.

Contents

by Bob Short

The way you walked was thorny though no fault of your own,
but as the rain enters the soil, the river enters the sea,
so tears run to a predestined end.

(The Wolfman, 1941)

ONE

The Wild West End, London, 1979

Was it the best of times or was it the worst of times? Maybe it was a bit of both. No. Surely, it was just the worst of times. It was 1979, a year that never could have imagined itself eulogised by the Smashing Pumpkins fifteen years on. Punk maybe wasn't so much dead as starting to smell decidedly iffy. Maybe one could be charitable and say it was not deceased but merely sleeping. New blooms were preparing to germinate. They were just taking their sweet time about doing it.

London was a turd placed strategically on the rim of a cesspit and lurking on the horizon, like some overwrought horsewoman of the apocalypse, was one *Margaret Thatcher*.

At least she'd ditched the high-pitched shrill voice she'd used in the past for a more rehearsed dulcet tone. Public Relations Training can work wonders.

You could almost taste the coming nuclear winter on the breeze. It came with hints of lavender like your least favourite aunt. The one who thinks she's posh and sticks her pinkie to the sky when sipping tea.

Slaughter and the Dogs had wondered where all the boot boys had gone but you didn't have to look far to answer their query. They're out there in your bloody audience. Those bouncing bald heads writhing at your feet. That's them. The church of latter-day brown shirts.

The sixties and their pretence of counter culture had fizzled under the weight of all that smoke and mirror, groovy baby, sexist bullshit. The pendulum had swung to the far right. Greed was on the ascendancy. One step forward, two steps backwards, baby.

It didn't help that London is a city that has deep roots. It's old. Older than Jesus. It's got ghosts. Hell, some of the ghosts have ghosts. That's why the rents are so high.

Someone has died in every room and on every street corner. Sometimes, their presence is so obvious you can very nearly touch them. If you are not careful, it's even been known for them to touch you.

And that's what drags in the tourists. Everyone loves a good haunting. It presents the punter with the possibility of immortality rather than the darkness of the endless void.

Walk those streets long enough and London kind of gets into your head like a fever dream. The High Streets melt together like a Cockney themed movie car chase. You know the one. Car turns left off of Whitehall, runs down an alley in Surrey Docks and end up on Tower Bridge. Then you're suddenly driving past Marble Arch.

Live long enough and you'll see the faces of old lovers now worn by children.

Live long enough and you'll see dead parents reflected in midnight shop windows.

It is thus unsurprising just how easy it is to take a sidestep down the wrong alley and find a parallel world.

It's a big town with millions of stories each with at least two sides and usually more. No wonder the centre cannot hold. As they say, nothing is true and everything is permitted. Except when you get unlucky.

My mother often dropped a lot of random superstitions and tales of the supernatural in odd and unsuspecting places. A kind of working-class white voodoo; part witchcraft, part Christian and part what the actual fuck.

Her parents had been seaside entertainers with a sideline in alcoholism. She didn't say much about them but I'm guessing that, at some point, at least one of them had been running a sideline clairvoyance hustle.

They had sent her to an orphanage when they went off to find the bottom of a bottle with the kind of minstrel show that came complete with boot polished faces and fake Southern American drawls. They just packed off and vanished while she was at school; the stuff of unpleasant fairy tales.

And the Hoodoo remained, entrenched in the cross generational trauma; tangled in the DNA. Passed down like a virus in the language. A concept here and a nonsense there.

Our personal civilisation built upon the quicksands of imperfect ancestry.

I had come down to the Crossroads. A hundred years ago, they used to say if you sat in Piccadilly Circus long enough, you would see everyone of import in the world. Over optimistically, I had come to meet the Devil (or at least one of his representatives).

The spider's web of tunnels leading from the tube station to the streets above offered a multitude of vices. Boys could be purchased in one, heroin in another. One path led to barbiturates but I felt the need for speed.

The Devil was a cash on the nail Prometheus mother fucker. Dressed all in black. Winkle picker shoes but no big fucking straw hat. Three for a quid. You paid your money and you took your chance and sold your dreams for revelation.

There was some vague promise of secret knowledge that could be acquired. There was even a vague perfume note suggesting fame and fortune carried on the aroma of stale subway urine. Not so much a guarantee as a whispered invitation to a dark laneway in a bad part of town.

Those little blue pills, they were just the commercial end of the deal. Off on some interconnecting fifth dimensional plane, deals were made and souls traded. The Fates weaved new threads.

Tomorrow would be a long time coming. Or a short time. Or not all.

Some people will tell you that *Charlie Parker* couldn't play anything worth shit when he wasn't on the gear. Others will tell you that the glory of the *Pogues* springs solely from *Shane MacGowan's* raging alcoholism. At the very least, we can all agree that *Nick Cave* hasn't made a decent album since he straightened himself out. These three statements are both gospel truths and utter fallacies. It's all in your interpretation. Drugs are neither good nor bad. They, like the continents floating upon the Earth's mantle, merely are.

That metaphor is not randomly chosen. So much of our popular culture rides on the back of trends in abuse. We make the music that the chemicals tell us to.

Speckled blues were a cheap kind of speed but no one knew what was really in them. Some people said they were chicken hormones, whilst others talked of strychnine. The one thing I know for sure is, even to this day, I can't enter a freshly bleached toilet without that smell opening a portal to the guilty pang of memory. That should provide you with a worrying footnote on chemical composition.

Years of speed psychosis would eventually leave us paranoid and wretched. We were always watched. Conspiracies abounded. Philosophies rose and fell in the course of an evening.

Charged by my Devil's unholy communion, I would dedicate myself to writing songs that, in the cold light of the morning, looked like the work of a psychopath. Quantity is no mark of quality. I would pull out notepads filled with last night's lyrics and they looked disturbingly similar to *Jack Nicholson*'s writing in *The Shining*. All work and no play made a decidedly dull boy. Forests were cleared as reams of paper filled with bad rhyming couplets.

They prescribe speed for ADHD and it is true it helps you focus. The trouble is you focus like one of those shit for brains normie neurotypical fuckers. In that mind set, fight rhymes with night and dead rhymes with head and that's good enough for the dreariness of popular culture.

But there was hope. If an infinite number of monkeys could bang out Shakespeare on their infinite array of typewriters, surely, I could drag perfection from the aether given an infinite number of little blue pills. Particularly when the come down turned you into the most brutal editor in human history.

Ten thousand hours to perfect a skill? Had I not found a way to accelerate through time?

The sun rose and fell and rose once more. Sleep may not have been murdered but certainly it was maimed. The realms of dream and nightmare slipped through the wound, blurring the gaps between being conscious and unconscious. The real and the surreal.

And finally, there was the obelisk. Floating just outside the orbit of Jupiter. The terrible gravity seized me and I plunged into the vortex and the inevitable crash.

To sleep per chance to dream.

TWO

Romford, Essex, 1965

They say history is written by the victors but, generally, the well-heeled losers at least make it to the footnotes in an attempt to make the winners look better. But the great unwashed merely see history as that which tramples them.

No one is taking notes and the names of history's victims. If we're lucky, there's a body count. When I was young, we mocked older people's obsession with the second World War. I am now writing about things historically more distant to now than the War was to them at the time.

My father's history was murky. His parents had washed up from Ireland in the early 1920's, settling in Wapping on the London Docks. They clearly had not told him of why that journey had been made and what had come before. He suspected the Potato Famine even though that had occurred some seventy years prior.

I remember him queuing at a booth in a supermarket mall that promised to trace ancestry. It was an ongoing racket in the nineteen seventies. In the really old days, they would have consulted a crystal ball. Now they'll do you a DNA swab.

We were not history's victors. We are refugees from our history. They'll always be someone trying to make a buck out of your diaspora.

These charlatans consulted their tomes and told him Short was not an Irish name. They offered a variety of dubious possibilities and similar sounding names, suggesting it had been Anglicised. They pointed at a number of items he could purchase affirming these supposed clan connections.

My father had a Christian name and two middle names. A quick check of the Irish census found a house in County Antrim where those names repeated in a sea of generational word soup. The house was in the infamous Ten Roads down by Belfast Docks and the Shankhill Road. In the wake of the Easter Rising, Loyalist forces essentially cleansed the area of Catholics, Trade Unionists and undesirables. It was called the Belfast Pogrom.

From June 1920 through to June 1922, more than 500 people were killed in Belfast alone, 500 interned and 23,000 people were made homeless in the city, while approximately 50,000 people fled the north of Ireland due to intimidation. According to one contemporary source *'The street was a mass of brain matter and blood'*.

But for every mystery solved, yet more rise in their wake. My father certainly was no Catholic. Nor did he have any particular love of trade unions or left leaning politics. At heart, he shared the views of the Loyalists his parents had fled.

Born in the East End, he had strived to be more Cockney than Cockney. How much of this character was nature, nurture, rebellion or simple desire to fit in, I will never know.

He did, however, cease talking to his mother when a business they had entered into together went astray. Money had gone missing. Accusations of criminal behaviour on her behalf was muttered under breath. The talk of immigration began to firm.

Then again, as much as I presented as alien species to him, maybe he was an alien species to his parents. A story teller likes nothing better than straight lines with the odd curved ball to add spice.

Real life is somewhat messier.

He joined the Merchant Navy the moment he could. He was on the Russian Convoy in the war. His boat was sunk by U-boat attack. He ended up in the North Sea. Oddly, he often described this time as the happiest of his life.

My mother, too, suffered through war time, surviving a bombing raid in a bath tub. One can scarcely imagine the amount of trauma hidden an inch beneath the surface. But such was the world my generation grew up in. The expectation that we should walk on egg shells could not survive our hormones.

Returning to a bombed out East End, large sections of the working class were farmed out into Essex.

As post war Britain ticked into the 1950s, my father became obsessed by immigration from the former colonies, unhindered by any sense of irony. He listened to the speeches of rich men leading the poor and saw the threatened rivers of blood. And thus, it was decided our family should head to the Antipodes. If there was a place furthest from the glowing centre of the Universe, my parents would surely find it.

THREE

Covent Garden, London, 1979

Covent Garden Underground Station has a ridiculous 193 steps from platform to the street above. I knew them well because you had to climb them in order to bunk the fifteen pence fare. Additionally, repetitious activities often make me start counting. The fact that economic necessity demanded we bunk a fifteen pence fare should underline the poor state of our finances.

Across James Street, behind a façade of plywood and corrugated iron, was a huddle of old shops and offices awaiting demolition. London needed more hotel space for the rich. The slums had almost been cleared. It was determined that the poor should no longer offend the wealthy with their existence. The ghost of an adventure playground marked their passing. Where have all the urchins gone?

The well-heeled sighed in relief. Their handkerchiefs and pocket watches were now safe from the artful dodgers of this world.

The last eviction notices had been served and the wrecking ball was booked. All that remained was a motley crew of squatters awaiting the bailiff.

There was a carpet on the floor somewhere. A thick layer of dust had begun to accumulate long before the corporate world had deserted the building. The dead skin of long departed clerks laid strata upon strata; a terrible geology of grey lives lost to hand written black and red columns.

The squatters who had rushed to fill the void had done their best not to disturb this grimy shroud. These were punk rockers. Their reticence to disturb the debris was not political. It was not born of respect for historical ruins or fear of unleashing a new wave of the Black Death. Nor were these kids afraid of what lurked beneath. The truth was that these under class underdogs were too lazy to swing a broom and had no knowledge of such latter-day inventions as the vacuum cleaner. They were likely lads who would, in future years, look at the *Young Ones* on television and bemoan the lack of authentic squalor.

I should know. I was one of them. And you young whippersnappers might think you know a thing about degeneracy. You only know the suburbs of squalor. We were let loose upon the big city.

I had spent a week huddled in the detritus on the floor wrapped in a woollen army jacket. Consuming nothing but orange juice, I hoped I would somehow recover from what was surely the longest lasting and most severe speed comedown in all of human history. In retrospect, I'd probably contracted some virulent viral infection along the way but, you know how it is, we all like to blame the drugs. Perversely, it is more socially acceptable. After all, a speed comedown is not infectious and no matter how dreadfully charred your pot is, it's always a laugh mocking the kettle.

I looked out through the dust frosted window and saw *Garry Bushell* strutting self-importantly around the offices of *Sounds* magazine across the road. He looked like some fat bearded *Mussolini*. No doubt he was singing the praises of some bonehead band of stormtroopers from Canning Town. I very much wanted a sniper rifle for my birthday.

As I mused over a career in cultural assassination, all hell broke loose in the next room. Dave was in a heated discussion with some guy from Brixton whose name I never quite caught. I was probably not supposed to catch his name. Such was the code of the underworld.

They had spilt their fresh purchase of heroin all over the floor. Dave dived down and begun snorting up the carpet. After all, when you think about how many people's arseholes that stuff had been through just to get it into the country, a little thing like two hundred years' worth of carpet dust was not going to make that much difference.

I had been aware of heroin before but at a distance. I'd been in a band and our drummer, Noel, had a peculiar habit of falling asleep in chairs and vomiting with no apparent concern or discomfort. Once, mid-way through an unrecognisable cover of *Iggy*'s *'I've Got a Right'*, he had regurgitated on his snare drum just in time for the next drop of the stick. The rest of the band and the front row of the audience copped an unhealthy coating of badly chewed vegetables. I'd told him that he should see a doctor about that shit but later someone pointed out to me the real cause of the problem.

It was a couple of years later and I was a little less naive. Still, the sight of two guys running their noses through a half inch of dust in the hope of getting stoned was an eye opener. In fact, I suddenly felt an overwhelming urge to visit the public wash house and soap the filth from my body.

Yes, children. There was a time when there was so little plumbing in London that the poor had to bathe in specially constructed council facilities. Lines of cubicles filled with the drunk, the insane and the great unwashed. Even as the nineteen eighties drew near, they were still there with that reassuring bleach smell screaming speckled blues in my ears.

"Excuse me, mate. Can you spare ten pence so I can have a bath."

It was, perhaps, the most effective poncing line ever devised.

We were simple folk. Our needs were few. We subsisted on a diet consisting mainly of tea, chips and the bread rolls that could be stolen by the bag full from outside the cafés of Covent Garden. The Hare Krishna's were good for handouts but that meant having to chant. Worse still, they might send *Poly Styrene* out in a bid to convert you. Seeing the woman who once screamed "Oh Bondage, up yours" now dead eyed and smiling like an American chat show host made it difficult to keep the food down. This was definitely not what we sought from our rock and roll heroes.

Booze was pricey. It was something that needed to be scrounged, borrowed or stolen. In those days, there were always plenty of men who wanted to buy you drinks. Their intentions were entirely dishonourable but make mine a double.

Hey. Once Rohypnol and Mandrax have entered your pill regime, you are pretty much immune to the worst of their side effects.

A group of us walked the dark streets of London's West End. There was safety in numbers. There was Tony (of *Ripped and Torn* and *Kill Your Pet Puppy* fame), Dave (soon to be of the *Sex Gang Children*), Brett and me. Brett liked to finish any visit to a café by filling his teacup with loudly snorted mucus. Unsurprisingly, we were rapidly running out of establishments that would admit us through their doors.

We were just lucky that the late-night places were used to far darker beings than us.

A taxi pulled over and who should emerge but one *Pete Townshend* and associated minders. Here was a man failing dismally in his attempts to die before he got old. He had that unhealthy pallor derived from years of chemical abuse only made that much worse by the orange street lighting. We claimed that there was no *Elvis*, *Beatles* or *Rolling Stones*. But the truth was we felt that life style was not merely what we aspired towards. It was our destiny.

Now we could see it climbing unsteadily out of a black London cab. He kind of slopped out like a human puddle.

Seeing our approach, the legend's eyes filled with fear. Despite the pull of gravity, he retreated back into the cab at an unholy speed. A cowardly moray eel. These kids were definitely not all right. The vehicle roared off into the night. We hadn't even had the chance to ask him for a spare ten pence.

Harder drugs were the stuff of Velvet Underground vinyl and Beat novels. They were almost mythical.

It still cost a couple of quid to go to the Marquee and the Lyceum was never more than three sobs. The idea of spending twenty quid on an illicit substance was impossible! Especially when the dole office only paid you thirteen pounds ninety.

"Excuse us, Pete. Can you spare us a line?"

Unless your name was Dave (and fuck knows where he got the money), heroin and cocaine were fantastical substances that existed only in the world of Pete Townshend's taxi. Even now that was retreating in the direction of Piccadilly and the posh beyond.

We proceeded into that hamburger bar on the corner of Neal Street and Shaftsbury Avenue. No sooner had the nosh been served up than Dave promptly face planted into a plate of chips and tomato sauce. He must have at least sucked some of that gear up with the house dust. As we pulled his head out of his meal, there was literally a single scarlet dipped chip wedged firmly up his left nostril. None of the drugs we had been taking up to that point could make you do that. We took the piss but I know that, deep down, I (for one) was secretly impressed.

FOUR

Fairy Meadows, New South Wales, 1966

We washed ashore in the great south land and were immediately herded onto a convoy of buses. No expense had been spent upon these vehicles that seemed to have been retired from suburban bus routes some decades earlier.

The hard seats rattled through the night, jarring bones and denying all hope of sleep. As we travelled South down the highway, darkness consumed us. There were no street lights and even less passing traffic. It was as dark as it gets.

The bus shuddered along with all the speed and grace of a milk float. (Younger readers might need to consult the internet.) On the straights we may have hit thirty-five miles per hour. Up hills, maybe twenty at the most.

I first saw Wollongong from the top of Bulli Pass. Far below us was a carpet of sodium vapour lights spread like embers of the netherworld and beyond lay the flames of Port Kembla Steelworks. It's hellscape appearance was amplified by the long and winding descent down the pass which included a particularly poor back and forth negotiation of a hairpin turn.

Asthmatically, the bus wheezed and panted to negotiate the turn. Someone actually had to get out of the bus to ensure the driver didn't tumble off the edge of the road and into the black abyss beyond. The rear axle became terribly close.

"You can come back another six inches!"

I became increasingly aware that this was an unusual position for a five-year-old to be in.

We arrived at the camp with the Eastern horizon tinting red with the approach of the sun. Row after row of tin Nissan huts greeted us on arrival; like something the Nazis had set up for a prisoner of war film. A communal shower block stood in the gap between rows, a larger hut housed the dining area.

There were no fans or respite from the heat. The afternoon sun was merciless on the tin roof. What followed was months of sweaty fever dreams as every imaginable child hood disease, influenza and gastro-tract infection followed the Ouroboros viral chain through the camp.

It seemed as though I spent months staring at the hallucinations that ran across the ceiling. But who could trust time when reason was lost?

FIVE

Old Street, London, Summer 1979.

The song was right. I had gone down to the Crossroads. It was inevitable I would get down on my knees. There are always plenty of folks ready to kick your legs from out under you.

I read the arcane literature of *Anton LeVay* and *Aleister Crowley* seeking an interpretation of the divine not born of fascism. It was important to engage the real world and politics. But the solution needed a transformation of self as well.

I took my volumes of scribbled notes and cast them inside a crucible. Fire burned away the impurities and excess.

I welded and, where necessary, bent words to fit melody. I composed secret chants and called them choruses. It took time but my grimoire of song was becoming complete.

Be careful what you evoke and invoke.

How many times have you got to be told? You steal fire from the Gods and there's going to be consequences. Or in simpler terms, there's no such thing as a free lunch.

Phrase it in any terms you want. It's the same shit with a different smell.

Most importantly, be prepared. When a line is crossed you may still return. But you're going to bring some things back with you.

Initially, it's the lesser demons that just follow you around the periphery, reminding you that you've got bills to pay. They try to keep you on edge with a constant darkening of your doorstep.

Later on, they'll raise the stakes with demonic possessions and zombie incursions. There'll be fire and pitchforks and cries in the night. The wailing and the gnashing of teeth.

You don't believe me, gentle reader? Then read on. My tale might seem tall but it's all true.

Summer was coming and the daytime stretched out to implausible lengths. It has something to with latitudes and the tilt of the Earth. Vampires fled southward, starved of opportunity. The sun set at ten and returned at three. And with every degree of rise in temperature, the streets got an inch more insane as brains boiled in their skulls.

There was that ongoing rise of bad intent and loss of patience. This would be no Summer of Love. Testosterone mixed with stale beer and, what the hell, the whole world was heading to hell anyway so no rules applied.

Thatcher cackled in the background, letting slip her dogs of war. She appealed to the working class for votes whilst stealing from their pockets.

The eighties towered before us, abased by the greed of the stock broker class. It was the birth of the trickle up economy as we fought over pennies in the dust.

With no football to distract them, the scrape knuckle brigade sought out victims on the highways and byways. Justified by their conceit of race, their poor education and a total lack of class, they howled for the return of a lost England they conjured out of dreams of cricket on the village green and piss weak tea.

They would hate it if that dream was made flesh and they had to live there.

Bottles smashed and knives were pulled. Western Civilisation attempted to end itself in one last almighty bar fight.

As seasons changed so did the drugs. The speckled blues dealers vanished overnight as if swept up in one huge bust or, at the very least, a highly targeted Rapture. The Dexys and purple hearts that briefly came to fill the void were poor substitutes that lacked sufficient kick. The black bombers and the sulphate were more expensive and more difficult to procure. It didn't matter. The world was changing on its axis, anyway.

With the rise in violence and constant threat of squat invasion, stimulants lost much of their charm. The quest for a new high became the search for a new low. Already, we had been learning to lessen the severity of our comedowns with Valium, Mogadon and, ultimately, Tuinal.

It was becoming obvious People wanted to kill me. This was not paranoia. These people wanted to kill everyone like me. In fact, anyone who wasn't like them.

Well, by people, I mean skinheads and, no, I'm not being metaphorical. These bone-headed bastards really were on a kill crazy rampage. Now fueled up on glue inhaled via crisp bags, the boot boys of yore made nightly raids on the punk squats of London. With peculiar visions of swastikas running through their heads, they staked out their claims to new Polands through rape, pillage and plunder.

"Night of the living Dead" was viewed as an educational film about how to keep the undead hordes at bay. Lesson one was to not do what the besieged victims of that film did. Nailing boards to doors and windows has little effect if the nails are hammered at a ninety-degree angle to the wall. The invading horde will merely push forward to minimal resistance. Nailing at a forty-five-degree angle... that was the ticket.

The police were watching me too. They wouldn't be strip searching me every day unless they were watching me, could they? Even when they weren't strip searching me, they strip searched me with their eyes.

It was probably good that they were watching me because, if they weren't, the skinheads would just be able to kill me there and then. Not that the cops would care. There would be paperwork and allegations of negligence didn't help your rise through the ranks.

Despite this overwhelming atmosphere of paranoia, I wasn't delusional. I cannot be any clearer, these fuckers really were out to get me with drugs or without. I thought I'd take the former option, thanks.

Taking drugs is like going to Disneyland. You start off by saying that it's a nice place to visit but you wouldn't want to live there. However, the minute you get back to the real world you want to go back to Disneyland. This is particularly true when the real world has become somewhere you'd rather avoid at all costs.

I found I could get the cops to leave me alone if I carried a bottle Quellada lotion in my top pocket. Quellada is a thick foul-smelling liquid used in the war against scabies and pubic lice. When the cops saw a bottle of that in your pocket, they didn't want to touch you with a ten-foot barge pole (rubber gloves included). It made the procurement of illicit substances that much easier but the trouble was, the more illicit substances you procured, the more the cops wanted to search you.

The days began to blur, first around the edges and then into one another. If I stayed awake for 32 hours and then slept for 16, I could live for twice as long. I wasn't just living better through chemistry; I was living faster. I was travelling through time. Suck on that, *Einstein*.

And you should have seen how thin I was getting. Look at my works, you super models, and weep.

I remember days where I don't remember anything. I can

remember walking out the door with a hand full of pills and suddenly I'm in a fight with an American tourist in Sloane Square. It happens with the quick snip of a Hollywood edit. The lights go off and when they come back on it is three days later. I'm in some godforsaken underground station at the top of the Northern Line. Kids, let me tell you something. Don't try that at home. I was a dedicated professional who had, by this stage, trained extensively to reach this level of degradation. What happened in those three days? I don't know. I don't want to know. I was having the time of my life and I was wasting my life. Both concepts seemed equally valid.

Unsurprisingly, few great symphonies have been written under the influence of Valium. Fewer great novels have been born of barbiturate overdose. There are no great paintings born of these drugs and, with the possible exception of the *Pogues' 'Old Main Drag'*, no great songs. Life on downers quickly turned into a numb routine of begging, petty shoplifting and half-hearted sex. One might start off wild, willing and wanton but, as the drugs kicked in, you would pretty much become soft, soggy and sleepy. You could walk into a room and look down at a cast that would not seem out of place in a renaissance tableau of the underworld. Instead of running in fear of your life, you would simply pull up a blanket and join them.

But sleep meant the absence of fear and that was a blessing to be embraced.

Out near (what seemed like) the wilds of Old Street, we moved into a new squat. The Fire Station on Tabernacle Street was a five-story building enclosing a central courtyard. Most of the upper levels were coated in a snowy white covering of petrified pigeon droppings.

If we had been in the South Pacific, indigenous miners would have been chipping away at the veritable fortune that was to be had.

But none of us knew that the economy of some islands was based entirely on the collection of petrified guano. More importantly, we knew no-one to sell it to.

Downstairs was a very large basement where some amps were set up at one stage. This basement may have descended a further two or three floors but I can't remember if I dreamt that labyrinth up or not. Life can get a little weird when you mix chemistry, trauma and rumour. I certainly remember a stairwell descending into the kind of darkness you'd do your level best to avoid in a horror movie. If it was real or not, who can say?

There was a point where the power ran out and I can't remember venturing any further into the pit.

It wasn't a completely punk squat; there were a variety of other miscreants to hang around with. The media may have told you that punks hated hippies but punks had a lot more in common with hippies than we did with the media.

On one of the first days I was there, a mad artist came running out into the courtyard; naked and with penis half erect (hand primed to make more of an impression). He threw his canvases into a massive pile and proceeded to set them alight in a grand statement that deserved a bigger audience. Dreams curled into ash and ascended the makeshift chimney between buildings. He was nimble and he was quick but I still suspect he singed his ball hairs as he leapt over the pyre.

I believe the artist's girlfriend had just told him his work was shit or something similar to shit. He departed that evening and one can only imagine which bank or insurance agency he went on to devote his life to. There but for the grace of God go we all.

There was Steve on the ground floor running some kind of illegal car repair shop and Ray who took photos. There were a couple of would-be metal monsters planning the return of the fifteen-minute drum solo and there was Gus who seemed to planning on becoming Buddha at some point.

On the punk side, Tony, Brett, Dave and I were the old guard joined by yet more reprobates. There was Val and Mitch, Jem, Lee, Lou and Ruthless. There was also this mad little Scottish kid named Gordon whose entire raison d'etre seemed to be taking whisky bottles he had emptied, refilling them with his own urine and leaving them on the step in the vague hope that somebody might be stupid enough to drink it. He endlessly hid in corners, awaiting his trap to be sprung by some unsuspecting *Godot*. It never was. His giggling was a dead giveaway.

There were others too but time has robbed history of their names; the wild, the beautiful and the damned.

One dreary Saturday afternoon, we all decided to sniff glue which – in retrospect – seems an absurdly stupid thing to do but it was a Saturday afternoon in Old Street and all the shops were closed. It was hardly the entertainment centre of the world.

We had already dropped a defunct television set off of the roof and watched it implode on the courtyard below as the vacuum tube shattered. This had made a fairly impressive noise so we decided to dump a dead gas cooker from the fifth-floor balcony. Its impact had made the entire building shudder. Even at the top of the building, I had felt the shock wave in my legs. Such excitement had demanded escalation and the freshly discovered pot of Evo-stick seemed to demand our attention.

The perceived experience of sniffing glue is rather different to the image the glue sniffer projects to the outside world. Walking past the drooling, collapsed form of the sniffer at play, one can only speculate on how a human could fall so low. A sniffer could never picture him or herself as that gurgling floor bound wreck. To sniff glue is to enter into the most vivid of dreams whilst maintaining a self-delusion of consciousness.

One of the most interesting hallucinations glue can cause is a delusion of shared experience. As eyes remain open, the hallucinations tend to include physical surroundings including the people around you. You therefore become convinced they see what you see because, in the dream, they converse and interact with you.

I'll be straight with you. There are a whole lot of ways to open the doors of perception. Solvent abuse is not an advisable course to take. There is too much medical evidence of brain damage, not to mention unpleasant fatalities and the fact it makes you smell really bad. I am lucky enough to be able to share my stupidity with you but, having been somewhere dangerous, in the cause of science and the spirit of discovery, it is necessary for me to report on what I have found there.

In this case, the report reads "Do Not Enter."

Reality continued its downward spiral. Even when sober, concepts drawn from this derangement of the senses found application in the straight world. For example, a vividly imagined telepathy made the concept of telepathy that tiny bit more plausible than it otherwise may have been.

Adding to this derangement of senses, I was hitting the occult text books pretty hard as well. I'd been brushing up on meditation techniques, astral projection and starting up a dream diary. One of the major effects this had was making my dream life incredibly vivid. With dreams becoming more real and reality becoming more dreamlike, the entire nature of reality was falling into question.

I woke up in the middle of the night imagining calamity in the floors below. Having heard what sounded like a German tank division coming through the front door, I got out of bed to see what was happening. There was nothing happening.

There was a large crash behind me as part of the roof collapsed and fell on my bed. I doubt this would have killed me but it would have hurt like a bastard. This was a real event that appeared to go far beyond simple luck. The world was turning weird in ways no chemicals or their abuse could explain.

What was real was the violence of the Summer of 1979. Skinhead violence had moved on from being a mere extension of terrace violence and racist bashings into what amounted to a criminal lifestyle. Punks were pretty much considered fair game for street robbery because the police were never called in. As I had discovered two months earlier, even if you were hospitalised, the interviewing officers they were obliged to send out merely spent twenty minutes taking the piss out of you. Cash was skinhead's immediate objective but unpainted or uncustomised leather jackets were easily resold. I even heard of boots being taken.

Was it a coincidence that punk fashion went totally post-apocalyptic at this time until pants became little more than layers of shredded rags from a variety of tattered garments worn one atop another until skin was (mostly) covered? Whilst no High Street fashion chain leapt upon this latest street fashion, at least no-one would try to steal them from you in the street.

Who would have guessed such distressed garments would become essential to the early twenty-first century fashionista?

Skinheads would "storm" small grocery stores; entering a premises and taking what they wanted from shelves through speed and numbers. Asian shop keepers were especially targeted for obvious political and racist motives.

It was not as if we were averse to a little shoplifting and petty theft but our techniques did not involve violence or menace.

Graffiti was, by accident or design, a potent terror weapon. The more skinhead graffiti you saw, the more likely it was that you would run into a group of these bald-headed freaks. Were the COD (Cash on Delivery) Skins an unstoppable army or two guys with a lot of spray cans? As the paranoia grew, who could really say?

British Movement Skinheads began specifically targeting *Crass* gigs at around this time. The audience, as opposed to the band, seemed to be the target of choice. At the Waterloo Community Centre, a group of around twenty to thirty skinheads entered the hall and drove a wedge through the crowd until they reached the point where the crowd became too thick to push forward. At this point, they turned and started throwing punches, quickly clearing the back of the venue. There had been a fairly large crowd in the Community Centre; probably around four of five hundred people. In the space of under a minute, the skinheads had bought the number down to about a hundred.

Once again, the skinheads turned towards the band and started laying into the audience at the front of the stage. If the objective had been to take the stage, destroy equipment and bend the band over the busted speaker cabinets, they could have easily achieved their goal. Instead, the target was obviously the crowd.

It wasn't as if they were fighting back. There was too much shock and panic to organise any kind of legitimate resistance.

Meanwhile, the band were threatening to go off stage if we didn't stop fighting. There was the usual tired rhetoric about *"us all being on the same side."* This was no doubt true in text book terms and *Ghandi* would have been proud. However, non-violent resistance is ultimately only effective against an enemy with a conscience even if it is a deeply concealed one. More importantly, we were not on the same side.

The Eagle Club, was a bare room in a Soho basement that tried to pass itself off as a night club. Later that night, many of the same characters from both skinhead and punk camps who had been at Waterloo were in attendance. Weirdly, there was no trouble at all. One did, however, get the distinct feeling that the skinheads were in recruitment mode.

Fear is an excellent motivator. By creating a campaign of terror more easily joined than avoided, the political right was, consciously or unconsciously, recruiting in the same way it did on football terraces. I obviously suspect the former because, even though I believe Fascist ideology to be morally bankrupt, I do not believe that necessarily means its practitioners are congenital idiots.

The assault on the Waterloo Community Centre gig had been too well orchestrated to suggest any notion of random attack. Besides, as Sigmund Freud would have told you, if there is one thing an anally obsessed Nazi loves, it is organisation.

This violence escalated over the summer. The first rumours began to filter through of attacks on a punk squat in Camden. The story that was going around was that they had busted through the door and beaten everyone up. Then they had individually dragged each occupant into a room and sodomised them with a broom stick.

In this climate, fact and rumour became indistinguishable. Given the violence and evil that abounded, I had no reason to doubt the truth of this.

SIX

Wollongong, New South Wales, 1968

Wollongong lay eighty clicks south of Sydney or 52 miles in old money. It was a smallish city sandwiched between the Pacific and the Illawarra Escarpment. At the time, the common misconception was that Wollongong was an indigenous word meaning "Look, here comes the Sea Monster" as this was where the local tribes allegedly first sighted *Captain Cook's* ship "The Endeavor".

But it's safe to say the indigenous population did know what a boat was and records suggest they compared the ship to a giant pelican.

The suggestion that a sea monster may have arrived was, however, more ominously accurate. An invasive species had arrived. Two hundred years later that invasive species would still teach of Cook's discovery in school whilst ignoring the fact there clearly were already people living there

Wollongong is actually an indigenous phrase referring to the five islands that lie just off shore.

The migrant camp was in the suburb of Fairy Meadow. Fairy Meadow was famous for two things; the migrant camp and the unsolved kidnapping and murder of children. The instance of child kidnapping seemed of great concern to the whole Illawarra region. At school, we certainly considered this to be a more likely demise than shark attack or spider or snake bite.

School was deeply unpleasant. Perhaps, the worst thing to be was a British immigrant. According to the native-born whites, the Greeks and Italians, cursed with mysterious accents and a splash more of a Mediterranean complexion, couldn't help what they were. They were essentially off limits. On the other hand, English kids could have the Britishness beaten out of them and it was entertaining to do so.

The most important thing was to get sunburnt to blister point so you could get that wretched pallor off your skin. I remember watching one poor unfortunate kid being set upon by his companions.

"I was born here! I've just been on holiday," he cried.

His chief tormentor and Lord of the Flies merely commented. *"It's bad enough you've been there. It's like a disease."*

As the barely noticeable winter turned to summer, the bushfire came. The sky went black and burning embers fell from the sky. The entire escarpment was aflame; a mountain range of fire.

They rounded us all up in the school's main hall, sitting sweating on the floor. We looked to the teachers hoping they were in charge but they looked like animals caught in the spotlight of an oncoming car.

SEVEN

Deptford Fun City, London, 1979

Humans can be incredibly kind or incredibly cruel. They can also be incredibly disinterested. There are many times one's life falls in to the hands of other's foibles.

I wandered south of the river, encouraged to see *The Cuddly Toys* in Deptford yet not entirely sure of how one would return north at the end of the evening. I largely followed the notion that fate would find a way. I was young and felt invincible in the way only the young can. If all else failed, my feet would carry me in the direction I needed to go.

Regrettably, I found myself straying from the path.

I found myself in Watergate Street, which was not so much a street as a narrow alley leading down to the Thames. It was like some peculiar portal into the land of Jack the Ripper. It was quiet beside the gentle lapping of the river. It was so pleasant that I considered sitting on the steps and just watching the eastward journey as the water flowed towards the sea.

I then realised I was not alone and I was in trouble. Three youths approached me brandishing iron bars and other weaponry. Was that a knife? It was hard to see with the street light so distant. Their stated ambition was to kill me and throw me in the river. It occurred to me that *Kit Marlowe* had met a similar end not too far from here.

There is nothing quite like the feeling of an iron bar crashed across the top of your head. It goes right through you with a deep and hollow thud. My knees gave way under the blow, helpless and turned to rubber.

Blood was already flowing down my face and I could barely see anything.

I knew if I stayed on the ground, I would die so I stood up, a gore covered shambling monstrosity. I think my attackers were quite taken aback by their handiwork and that I had risen to my feet from the impact.

I copped what I thought were a few half-hearted blows to my limbs and side. I was pretty much passed all feeling. My hand was pumping out its life blood upon the cobblestones but I kept on walking.

I was not thinking, I was moving; placing foot before foot; my back to the river. A wounded animal, I was beyond fear and pain. I focussed on escape but I was beyond internal monologue. I directed myself towards the brightest lights.

Eventually, there were passersby fleeing in terror. I was a ghost of Christmas future, the embodiment of their night time fears. They too could end up like me. Finally, a restaurateur told me through hastily locked doors to sit on the pavement away from his shop whilst calling an ambulance.

Safely sat in the cold white light of Lewisham Hospital, many stitches followed. Shaved hair piled upon the floor as new wounds were uncovered. The police asked disinterested questions with no plans of arrest until the nurses chased them away.

Shock faded into abject horror and finally sleep arrived to rescue me.

EIGHT

A Season in Hell, 1971

The dog was getting overly nippy and bitey and I just didn't want to play that game. For fucksake. You know dachshunds. A mouth with too many teeth. Bred to fight badgers. I'm just trying to eat a goddamn sandwich and fur face wants to tax me. The more I push back, the more insistent he becomes, snapping at my fingers and digging away with those surprisingly vicious front paws. I decided to sit on the sideboard cupboard because that's what a ten-year-old does when they don't want to fight with a dog over a sandwich.

Now what could possibly go wrong? Apart from there being a metal desk fan beside me. And there was a metal light fixture on the wall. Not forgetting some long-forgotten idiot electrician who failed to grasp the concept of the earth wire. If something can go wrong, I often feel that I am the poor bastard who is going to find out exactly how that wrong is going to happen.

And then I was somewhere else. Like most people, I've seen my share of those cruddy articles in the Sunday papers that tell tales of going towards the light and being met in a garden by someone who has passed over before you. They are nice stories, clearly written more as a comfort for the living rather than any help to the dead.

"Am I dead? Is that all I get?"

I found myself shrugging in quiet acceptance.

I had every reason to believe that I was no longer of the living. The place I found myself was tangible and textured. I was more alert than I had ever been. This was no dream.

If there was any truth in those stories of a joyous afterlife, it was a truth not for my eyes. I was not destined for that land of perpetual summer's end. There was no sugar candy mountain that awaited me. I quietly asked myself what terrible sin could a child commit to earn such a cruel fate.

But this was not hell in any traditional sense of the word or image I had seen. The place where I arrived was as unexpected as it was strange. More passage than destination. Perhaps God was a surrealist made mad by his creation. That was as good an explanation as any I had at my disposal. There was no sanity in this greatest of follies.

My ears were filled with the insane laughter of clowns. I was going to say evil clowns but that goes without saying, doesn't it? It goes with the territory. You cannot skirt the edge of insanity without collecting a few bumps and scratches along the way. Some say beneath a clown's make-up, they are really crying. Give me a fucking break. Two words, people. Personality and Disorder.

I was on a rollercoaster ride. I'm speaking literally here. I'm not alluding to my experience being like the fairground ride with its ups and downs and twists and turns. Read my lips. Not a metaphor. I was on a real rails-of-steel, wooden scaffolding, throw up your candy floss rollercoaster. In fact, to paraphrase *Saddam Hussein*, I was on the mother of all rollercoasters.

Its peaks towered miles above its troughs. Those perilous summits would have been obscured by clouds if the red sky that enveloped this world had clouds. What was more to the point was whether or not the red sky could be described as sky at all. If blood was a gas and not a liquid, it would be blood that comprised the atmosphere through which I was moving. You could taste the iron in the air. I felt as though I was trapped in my own heart.

This gargantuan structure, upon which my carriage rattled along at a breakneck speed, was freestanding in the ruddy void. There was no division between earth and sky. Only the rollercoaster was there, hanging in a big red nothing.

The strangeness of my surroundings and the suddenness of my arrival had disorientated me. If the abyss had not been scary enough, my mind had just made something scarier. I had forgotten I had just died and the combination of vertigo and sheer terror stopped me remembering. The present was way too terrifying to think about little things like how or why I had found myself there in the first place. One thing was for sure - I was not enjoying myself one little bit as my carriage climbed upwards towards the impossible heights of an apex, let alone when I was plunging down the equally impossible descent that followed from it. I constantly felt as though I had left my stomach several miles back on the track behind me. What was left of my brain was lost further back still.

After being flung up and down for several lifetimes, the carriage reached the summit of the absolute Everest of all these peaks. It groaned against the steepness of the climb. Metal buckled under obscene pressure.

I could not draw breath in this rarefied atmosphere. Below me, the track vanished into a hole of utter darkness suspended impossibly in space. The carriage was tipping forward over the crest. Soon I would face that final dread descent that ended in nowhere at all. I knew that I didn't want to go there but that was all I knew. Teetering on that edge, I was beyond fear and beyond words. I was at the start of one long scream that would echo forever.

This was the most pregnant of pregnant pauses; less the quiet and more the sheer bloody terror before the storm. If I stayed still, could I just find balance?

Insanity was a living thing in my veins. It pumped madness with every pounding heartbeat. Boom, boom. Boom, boom. Boom, boom. A primal fear. A dread beyond all chance of hope.

The black hole hung at ninety degrees from all of reality and, like its namesake in outer space, it had a terrible gravity. It beckoned grimly and even the sky obeyed. The rush of bloody wind was deafening. It stripped my flesh of name and self. This was hell and it called to me.

Deep within the hole, there were no ups and no downs, no

yesterdays and no tomorrows. From my perch on the top of the rollercoaster scaffolding, it looked more lonely than life and the track led straight into its always hungry innards.

I had no brake, no means of escape and gravity was doing what gravity does best. The more I saw, the less I liked, the more I wanted to escape. Gravity had other ideas. It had all the will and determination of a destiny that would not be denied. Worst of all, it had all the time in the world.

NINE

Old Street, London, 1979

Of course, in the squats of Old Street, we had no luxuries such as television or radio. Wars could rage and disasters fall but we would be none the wiser. The posters for newspaper headlines were as close as we got to the real world. We were already in the gutter and, even as we attempted to glimpse the stars above, cloud cover denied us.

We sought out entertainment of our own. We laid out a large mirror on the table and drew a circle of letters in lipstick. An upturned glass filled with our breath sat in the middle awaiting the summoning.

Soon, the glass was flying beneath our communal fingers and it didn't take us long to raise the spirit of *Sid Vicious* (or SV for short and we filled in the necessary gaps.

The voice of the glass was insistent. Punks were under imminent threat of death. WAPS were coming to kill punks.

For years, I occasionally wondered what this meant. A new disease? A Government agency? A new youth fad? Whilst I never seriously considered any kind of real threat, there was that peculiar corner of my brain threatening to succumb to superstition.

Imagine my surprise when the term WAP finally entered the contemporary vocabulary. But it was true. What power did punk have to continue to offend in an era of wet ass pussies?

TEN

Figtree, New South Wales, 1971

I did not die. Apparently, if I'd weighed just a little more, I would have been a crispy critter hanging off the wall. Instead, the voltage threw me across the room. Somewhere along the way, I'd collided with a snooker trophy, the tiny cue tearing a seven-stitch gash in my cheek.

In my last moment in the other place, I had found myself inside a giant ballon, the pressure building until it hurt my ears. I pressed at the rubber walls, convinced of their reality. I was as awake there as much as I am here at this keyboard.

The balloon burst and I found myself on the floor. Having little understanding of electricity, I stumbled out into the garden to grasp the hills hoist in a desperate bid to cast out excess current.

I wandered into the street, trying to explain to the gathering crowd what had happened to me. But my experience had been too strange to be understandable. Giant rollercoasters. Railroads to hell. Giant balloons.

The more I said, the more people were certain I was in shock. It didn't matter how real the experience felt, what was important was that I accepted it as delusion. Someone was sticking a needle in my arm.

My last memory before passing out was a stranger telling me it was okay and you get over these things. He held up his hand to reveal two missing fingers. He told me with a smile he had accidently sliced them off with a machete whilst chopping sugar cane.

It was not conducive to feeling comfortable.

For the next few months, taunted by this vision of an afterlife, I began to seek God's forgiveness for whatever terrible thing I'd done to deserve such torment. I prayed. I read the bible. I copped a full emersion baptism in what amounted to a bathtub full of water.

Whilst submerged, I had a vision of Christ beside me. It felt incredibly fake. I came up from the water feeling an extraordinary clarity. This religion thing was complete bullshit. It was pure mass hysteria. It changed nothing.

ELEVEN

Kilburn, London, 1979

The autumn was setting in. Tucked in the salubrious streets behind Kilburn Station, St Monica's Hospital was established for one purpose and one purpose alone. As a neighbour bluntly put it, they wheeled them in through the front door on stretchers and took them out again through the back in boxes. It was not a place you went to recover unless it was life itself that ailed you. Wrapped in a flag of teenage angst and nihilist urges, we thought we'd give squatting it a go.

The place was due for demolition, making way for either a planned retirement community or a maximum-security geriatric unit, depending upon your viewpoint. Names often change but the Earth knows that there are places where you live and prosper and others where you go to die. Even elephants have their graveyards. It goes back to some forgotten knowledge never taught to man but sens   some way that is beyond mere language. At least that's wh.   this dealer guy told me when I went off scoring shit. He also believed in UFOs.

There may have well been a proclamation concealed within the architecture that demanded the abandonment of hope for all those who entered St Monica's but we ignored any such edict. It was no surprise that we chose to break the rules. Even carved in stone in massive letters, writ large on tablets bought down from the mountains, no-one was telling us what to do. If the rules were hidden from our eyes, that gave us even more reason to be stupid. Besides, it was the easiest squat that anyone had ever opened. There was no breaking required when it came to gaining entry. The door was wide open and we walked straight in.

Even if it had been barred and bolted, there were more than enough broken windows that you could have squeezed yourself through. A real estate agent would describe the place as a real fixer-upper. It kind of proved that old adage about living in glass houses in the most prosaic way possible, though it failed to mention the sheer entertainment value that such a venue could provide bored urban youth. Over the years, many a school boy had paused to throw stones at the old haunted hospital. It had become one of those little rituals to be passed through on the way to manhood.

Evicted from squat after squat, we were attracted by location, location and yet more location. Suburbia, with its quiet tree-lined avenues, had beckoned and we answered its call. Being far from the maddened throng of BM Skins, COD Skins and other assorted cropped freaks was a distinct advantage for those wearied by months of undeclared war. Our tube line was no longer their tube line. We learnt how to live without impending threat, imminent peril or even the accidental crossing of paths. It was better to sleep with the dead than live sleepless and in fear of the brain dead. You could call it a holiday.

That said, there was no running water, no electricity and the English winter could almost be seen on the horizon. In some Neolithic quest for body heat, we all set up home in a single room and sought the safety of numbers. The cold and the rapidly putrefying odour of unwashed clothes and bodies largely enforced a regime of celibacy. Given our close proximity, things were getting more than a little weird.

The powers that be wanted their real estate back. A court date had been set and the sheriff's men waited in the wings for the judge's gavel to fall.

Actually, they waited in their white transit vans drinking over stewed café tea and buns but that doesn't have the same ring to it. They need not have bothered. Their law meant nothing here. The whole venture was doomed from the beginning because the land had already chosen a time for our departure.

As that time approached, we increasingly found ourselves gripped by our curious neo-primitivism. Superstition became more than just an old *Stevie Wonder* song. If you took a certain stairway and your dole cheque didn't come, the two events became automatically linked and were recorded as omen. One set of stairs became lucky and another cursed. Survival was suddenly dependent on the observance of these patently absurd yet comfortingly fresh off the spectrum rules.

Of course, these rules didn't seem absurd at the time. If sanity is judged according to the standards of a society, a common psychosis becomes the norm. If society really wanted to help the delusional, the mental hospitals would be filled with the pious of all faiths, members of any of the political parties and anyone who studied economics.

We lived by candlelight and supernatural creatures constantly flickered at the periphery of such poor illumination. Dreams ceased to vanish upon waking. Reality became an option we often failed to observe.

The first Zoff trip set the tone for our adventures. In that one brief sentence, if you know what Zoff is, I have already told you more than you need to know. Zoff was a kind of liquid you bought in chemists to remove sticky plasters. You could also pour it on a sleave and inhale.

This brazenly cavalier attitude towards the lowest form of chemical abuse surely points us out as the kind of people you'd cross several roads in order to avoid. Do not be fooled by my well-crafted sentences. We were scum and many folks crossed many streets when we walked by. You need not feel alone in your disgust.

Jake was a middle-class kid who had stumbled in from a leafy neighbouring suburb because he wasn't like those other freaks. His band were called *The Heretics*. He was covered in a preternatural coating of grime that made his skin appear grey. His clothes hung like rags. A human statue, he had entirely crossed the line.

Pulling my face out of my sleeve, I looked across to see Jake's features twisted into something akin to the face of Pan. The only major variation on the classical interpretation was his four goatlike eyes that ran as two parallel tracks beneath his brow. They blinked randomly, as if upper and lower sets were possessed by different intelligences. I pointed him out to my fellow travellers and we all stared in amazement.

"You've got to see this."

"Oh what?" Ruthless gasped unprompted and pointed at Jake's face. *"You've turned into the devil."*

This unison of vision was inexplicable but I was not afraid. There was a fair chance that I was dreaming everyone's responses, anyway. Still, my curiosity was piqued by this derangement of the senses. Holy fool or plain madman, I would be master of this realm. Romantic notions of the shaman's path flitted through my teenage brow. Working in tandem with my unchecked desire to become as wasted as humanly possible, the end results would not be pretty.

Come the dawning, our less than merry band strayed onto Hampstead Heath in search of magic mushrooms. Without lights, radios or television, both bedtime and the old rise and shine came embarrassingly early. Waking to the crow of some imagined cock was accompanied by hunger and the desire to piss. Without access to water, an isolated corner in a distant wing was agreed on as the pit of ablution.

This was followed quickly by boredom, hunger and yet more boredom. That damn boredom just got everywhere. The hunger wasn't helping much either. When we were bored, we were really bored and, when we were bored, we would do just about anything. An idea involving mind altering chemicals would be leapt upon no matter how pathetic that idea was.

So, with our breath hanging cold in the air and vulgar songs spewing from our lips, we headed out into the mist in search of the rising sun and possible intoxication. The seven dwarfs go to Hell.

The drug fiend myth runs the line that the first mushroom is near impossible to find but once located and consumed, others will start calling out to you. Maybe that meant an increased focus and maybe it meant that we were picking up bits of whatever shit we could find and just thinking they were mushrooms. More likely, the myth was totally untrue. I have never heard any of the little fuckers calling out to me. I just haven't said anything about my doubts before in case people thought I was doing it all wrong.

Drug fiend myths are remarkably unreliable. My personal favourite used to be that Tuinal was a truth drug and, once consumed, you would be rendered incapable of lying. After an experiment revealed this as fallacy, I felt a sudden overwhelming urge to go Munchausen on everybody's arse. I only ever lied when I took Tuinal. If I ever told the truth whilst taking Tuinal it was only because I was too bored to keep playing my little game. Spearing fish in barrels gets old really quickly.

It took a bit of searching but our quest met with some limited success. As noon approached, we left the fields and moved into the wilder edges of the heath. We had a bit of a buzz on by then but the place was starting to fill up with dog walking pensioners and rosy faced children as yet unsullied by the horrors of the education system. The former spoke of inevitable cruel fate whilst the latter pointed at our own falls from grace. Basically, the buggers were bringing us down big time so we sought out some shadows where we could lurk undisturbed.

Amongst the trees, against the background of Autumnal debris, the fly agaric mushrooms grew. Because of their striking red colour, it is easy to be drawn to them whilst sober. They looked like they have been plucked from the pages of a Victorian book of fairy tales. *"Now that,"* you find yourself saying. *"That is what I call a magic mushroom."*

When you have a few hallucination inducing chemicals running through your frontal lobe, the effect is even stronger.

"Those things are poisonous," said Jess. She was always the voice of reason.

"Yeah," said Mitch. *"But aren't they the ones that witches used to take to make them think they were flying."*

This titbit of information was exciting. Our drug fiend ears pricked up in the same way dogs do when you reach for a can opener. I was fairly certain that they were supposed to have made a paste which they rubbed on their skin to achieve this desired effect but, if someone had a different story, I was prepared to go there. Especially if it meant getting wasted. Any knowledge I possessed on the subject came from Hammer Horror films and even I regarded that as suspect.

"I read about that," said Rick in a kind of way that made you think he had never read anything in his life.

Rick came from a long line of gung-ho liars. Him and his girlfriend Tammy claimed to come from sunny California. They actually came from some shit eating mid-western town but thought being Californian might actually impress us. They had clearly not overcome the culture shock of crossing the pond. We were punks for fuck's sake. California was where the shit settled when the sea formed a barrier against further westward migration. California was the home of swimming pools, movie stars and *Mickey* fucking *Mouse.* It should have been nuked accordingly.

This unlikely couple had come to our shores on a starry-eyed quest to find *Jimmy Page*. Apparently, they were the best of mates and the band always dropped by when they were in town. They claimed the Zep dude had invited them over but they had misplaced his address and phone number. As you do. Basically, they had this whole religious iconography thing going on and their weirdness had led the poor bastards to us. I have long given up seeking explanations for the strange paths that life leads us down. Applying meaning to madness is a fool's errand.

"To stop it being poisonous, they used to cook it in milk and strain it through muslin."

It sounded more to me like he'd heard of a way to prepare blow fish and confused it with a recipe for making pate. Removed from his televisual window on the world, I don't know where he was getting his information. The only logical explanation was that he plucked facts from out of his arse because he had nowhere else to hide them out of plain sight. That said, he did gain followers to his cause. The quest to get high forbids the lame excuse of common sense. Soon a carrier bag was filled with poisonous fungus and we left towards a date with something quite like destiny.

There would be rivers of vomit and unbearable abdominal pain. It was going to get biblical. There would be a wailing and a gnashing of teeth. There would be the flashing of lights and ambulance rides. Oh yes, there would be ambulance rides to yonder Neasden Hospital where the stomach pump resides. The dreams that would come would be drenched in terror's sweat instead of revelation. You know it and I know it and yet I keep on typing.

I'm like a bad comedian sometimes. I've given away my punch line and now I'm standing alone here in the lights, desperately trying to keep an audience from audibly groaning. A good writer would throw in a few plot twists to build the suspense or mask the play he was making. 'Tis a pity then that I am not a good writer. Like a clown who drops his trousers, I shall have to give it to you straight.

We'd keep milk in a bucket of cold water in some half-hearted bid to prevent it from turning into the giant yoghurt turd that was its inevitable fate. By the time we had returned, things had not deteriorated that far but the process of separation had commenced. Little specks of curd began to form out of the whey. That was okay. We were only going to use it to wash the poison out of mushrooms on the advice of a self-confessed artiste d'bullshite. Everything was fine. Bacteria were merely a con perpetrated by the manufacturers of antibiotics and disinfectant in order to raise revenue. Why settle for the awful truth when a well spun conspiracy theory works that much better.

Muslin presented another problem as no-one was going to surrender a Seditionaries Destroy shirt to the project. A Boy T-shirt was a different matter. Someone came up with a badly designed, thoroughly worn and never washed *Clash* shirt. Since they returned from America, we had labelled that band as traitors of the lowest order and would not be caught dead wearing their image. That garment would have to do.

There was a brief debate about the skin of the mushroom. There was one school of thought that said that the colour red was nature's warning and should be peeled and discarded. Others were sure that skin was where all the goodness lurked and you should never peel vegetables.

You can see for yourself how dangerous a little knowledge can be. The peelers won the day with a campaign speech that included all the heavy hitters. Better safe than sorry. If it doesn't work, we'll keep the skins and use them next. They had the better line in logic whilst the non-peelers relied on a more suspect hippy argument and that never went down well in the big city. Nutrition was just something you did when you had no access to sugar.

After leaving it to stand in an old baked beans tin for a while, we dropped the soggy mess of mushroom milk onto the back of the shirt and twisted it up into something like a bag. We continued to twist it more tightly until a foul coloured and fouler smelling liquid began to drip onto the floor. This putrid ooze was considered to be a sign of success. Surely a substance that vile proved all evil had been expunged from the mix.

Riding a wave of anticipation, we opened the package and examined the contents. I swear to you that I have seen more appetising diarrhoea. My compatriots came quickly to a similar conclusion. We did the only thing we could. We built a fire and commenced a fry up. After a time, the contents of the pan began to resemble regular fried mushrooms - which is to say they looked like blackened semi chunks of crap. A touch of salt. A splash of tomato sauce. Lovely Jubbly.

Rick decided to bring the appetite of your average American cowboy superhero to the table. Upon his broad shoulders lay the reputation of the home of the brave and the land of the all-you-can-eat buffet. Here was a man who had never seen a plate he hadn't scraped down to the enamel. Minutes into the future he would be giving Linda Blair's performance in the Exorcist a good run for its money. Now he was busy proclaiming to all and sundry that he had tasted of this work and all was good. Being a dutiful wife in training, Tammy followed suit.

An air of non-commitment was taking root in the native community. Whilst we wanted to see what would happen to the test patients before imbibing, the barn yard frenzy around the pan meant that by the time we had seen the result of our experiments the fruit of our labour might be lost to the ravages of colonial appetites.

The future held everything you may have expected.

The National Health Service. God, you have to love it.

TWELVE

Wollongong, New South Wales, 1973

I don't have many memories of kindergarten in Romford. Snow on the front doorstep. The climbing frame in the local park. The neighbouring kid taking a dump in a pedal car. A recurring nightmare about King Kong crashing through a wall. The usual stuff, really.

I don't actually remember being smacked in the face by a random twelve-year-old. I do remember sitting in the school's sick bay, covered in blood and being amazed by the swelling of my split lip and the sudden looseness of some of my teeth; the strange new geography of my face. But as small children, our life is a dream. Random images awaiting our brain to properly click on.

Other than that aforementioned attack, primary school was usually fairly easy to cope with on both sides of the world. If you have a little bit of smarts, you can negotiate playground politics because children have yet to discover the advantages of dishonesty. Cruelty, generally, is learned. It is, however, a seed that flourishes once sewn.

In those early years, the academic requirements are not exactly taxing. It doesn't take much effort to answer a teacher's questions. How do you spell cat? What is two plus one?

You can also suck at sport and no-one cares.

One particularly strong memory involves first grade at Wollongong Primary School. Even at six, I remember walking to school alone. This was how things were done. I can even now remember seeing rays of light beaming through tree leaves and sea mist. I sat in the playground as my mind seemed to just turn itself on as if a veil had been lifted; an experience more profound and psychedelic than any drug trip.

Of course, it wasn't all without incident. I was about eight the first time someone put a knife to my throat. Walking down an alley to Sunday School (of all places), I saw two of the older boys generally lurking. The next thing I know, I was up against a wall with a point of a blade pressed under my chin.

"If you tell anyone about what we were doing, I'll kill you."

The sad thing was, I didn't have a clue what they had been doing. I'd barely noticed them. I would have walked right past entirely unaware of whatever vice they were indulging. Yes, people have bad things happen to them for the dumbest of reasons. People could be savage but, that time at least, I walked away with minimal damage and with no sense of fear. I was quietly protected by an idiot notion that shit just happens. Just like on television.

Later on, I would be further protected by being sent to an OC (opportunity class). At the time, this was considered a way to raise the gifted and talented up to be the cream of the country's future. We were told we could do anything and be anyone. Clearly, the choices I made would not be what they had in mind.

The OC class was also an ideal environment for the neurodiverse and, at the time, the entry exam seemed targeted to seek us out. These days, people pay tutors to prepare their children to answer questions we had considered a fun game. The notion that being "gifted and talented" can be taught maybe calls into question the entire concept. If it is really so advantageous and can be taught, why don't they just teach everyone?

My best friend at school was Peter Raengel. If anything, he may have been further along the spectrum than me but, then again, maybe not. Many years later, I would learn that he had gone on to form a band called the Sunday Painters that featured a number of other of my ex-classmates. They essentially thrived in the isolation of the Steel City.

The strange thing was that how, even as ten-year-olds, we sparked against each other. We wrote comics and plays in a kind of way that competition and collaboration blurred, each trying to outdo the other. Through each other, I think we could both take our obsessions with monsters and weirdness and somehow make something like art although I suspect neither of us had any idea what that meant at the time. This was the great adventure mimicked in every art scene ever. Giants are born in battle with other giants.

In life, we crash into each other. The dangerous sparks of these interactions build strange new worlds. That which makes us different to everyone else is our greatest strength.

Essentially neurodiversity is not a bad thing. Whilst ADHD has the disadvantages of burn out and overload, it has the glorious super power of hyper focus.

There is, however, a large chance of having autism as a comorbidity. This brings with it difficulties in forming relations and obsessive ritualistic behaviour bordering on self-inflicted superstition as you may have noticed in previous chapters.

There was a time I could not successfully leave the bathroom without pressing a series of tiles in a correct order. This ritual seemed to be developing exponentially in line with increased stress. I believe the kids call it stimming but I was entirely unaware that this was in anyway divergent behaviour. With its wilful brutality, the world was clearly not so much wild at heart as it was weird on top and it appeared to get weirder still if you dug deeper down towards its core. In this light, how could my experience be outside any norm?

In hindsight, I realise I had bizarre notions that selecting certain times could produce better results based solely on some mysterious quirk of numerology. There were potential dangers of interactions involving engagement with various numbers. Paths needed to be followed exactly down to each and every footfall.

Initially, I attempted to work on defeating these notions with attempts of serious doses of logic but this method proved ineffective. Soon I would embrace rashness and danger to much greater success. It was, perhaps, for the best that I was removed from the broader stream of public education.

Unfortunately, the OC was a primary-school based project and when the time came, we were cast back into regular high schools, in my case in Figtree. The first problem was becoming accustomed to the boredom. Not only did you find yourself asked to repeat work you had completed years ago, you were suddenly surrounded by kids struggling with work you'd completed years ago.

Sport formed a large part of this world and I was baffled as to why it seemed to suddenly hold such sway over the masses. What was this invisible star they sought to orbit? I looked to the sky and saw nothing.

The students who did best under this regime were those who learned by rote. If you asked the question *"Why?"* teachers met you with blank disdain. They didn't know why. They just read the fucking text book. Most of them were PE teachers forced to lecture on science.

The actual PE teacher seemed overly obsessed with bending boys over his knee and delivery a dubious form of justice involving a table tennis bat. He was squat and round and simply blowing a whistle turned his face red and caused him to lose breath.

The metalwork teacher had a personal atrocity exhibition involving hair and scalp caught in drill bits and photos of all manner of industrial injuries. Metalwork, he insisted, was not meant for sissies.

But the worst thing of all was that so many of the kids had just grown to be plain mean with the rise of testosterone and estrogen levels.

Teachers hid in their staff rooms, casually day drinking. If you know the smell, you know the smell and certain educators over indulged. By close of day, the breath, the slur and the bleary eyes had a certain intense obviousness and still the six o'clock swill was calling. After all, it was the Nineteen Seventies.

There were more than a few Vietnam veterans who had survived their conscription only to sail into a sponsored teacher's degree. Their thousand-yard stares proved indifferent to anything under their noses. One told a tale of adding potassium permanganate to ammonia and letting the mix set on a superior's seat. Careful, children. Don't try that at home. Though I suspect, through accident or design, this guy didn't know the difference between ammonia and sulphuric acid.

This was a prison without guards. The brutalist style of architecture provided few line of sight views. Shadowy passages harboured many dangers. The toilets and the lockers were absolute no-go zones even if you could withstand that unique schoolboy stench. The most brutal flies fought for control. One time, the police were called in only to have their van over run and the door of the locked box torn asunder to release their newly claimed prisoner.

Every morning at assembly, we heard the same unbelievable line. "We know who you are. Don't make us come and find you." They literally found no-one in the entire time I was there. No-one named their perpetrator. To report a bully would bring the wrath of the whole school down upon your head.

And this is just how the teachers wanted it. Divided, we were conquered. If we were killing each other, they could sit at their desks smoking cigarettes, drinking instant coffee laced with their not-so-secret Johnnie Walker Red Label and waiting to retire as soon as was humanly possible.

In May, the rains would come. Mighty storms broke against the escarpment and the deluge would burst the creeks but, if God had wished to wipe all evil from the land, he would need to send more water. The sports fields that surrounded the school would vanish beneath the churning grey flood waters. When this occurred, you would not be going to school that day. Or the day after and sometimes not the day after that.

One year, the carcass of a drowned cow was left twenty feet up a tree. Stranded high up in the branches, no workers came to drag it down. It may have been the end of autumn but the Australian sun did what it did best. It beat down unrelentingly and the corpse grew like a balloon. There was not so much a halo of flies as a veritable Oort Cloud.

Eventually, a student had the bright idea of targeting the remains of the beast during javelin practice. Once pierced, the smell was unbelievable, carrying for miles and clinging for days until the birds and the insects vanished it away.

The school's motto was and remains *"Crescere Fidere*

Statuere" (To Grow. To have faith. To stand firm). Of course, we had no Latin teacher so no-one knew what these words meant. The only language teacher we had was Miss Ellis. She quit when someone defecated in her desk drawer.

Perhaps they should have gone with "Spes *hic Moritur*" (Hope Dies Here).

THIRTEEN

Kilburn, London, Halloween 1979

I spent many days in the grounds of St Monica's awaiting Halloween whilst hunting rabbit. I swear I could see many of the little guys moving through the undergrowth and my startled fascination turned quickly to obsession. The only rabbits I had ever seen were in butcher shop windows. Many were the times I'd chuck a *Captain Ahab* over some new idea or another and this would prove no exception. A dream is not a dream until you have gone down with the ship over it.

I set up a large cardboard box and raised one side with a stick. A length of electrical wire torn from the walls ran between the stick and my makeshift hide. In the bitter cold, I waited. Though it took day and night and day again, I would catch one of these wee beasties. Whether he was made of flesh and bone or less tangible matter, his little cotton tailed butt was mine. I did not know if I would eat him or adopt him as a pet. I was conflicted in my agenda but that didn't stop me setting the trap regardless. Like *Elmer Fudd*'s quest for the elusive *Bugs*, my enterprise would meet with all the success it merited and that was none at all. I at least had the excuse of being deranged to fall back on. Poor *Elmer* was just a dick.

As the nights imperceptibly lengthened, a kind of sanity seemed to settle over the place. We took to the safe oblivion of alcoholic beverages. We may have taken other forms of abuse just a little bit too far.

In the mornings we would go to a pre-determined street corner and a van would collect us. We would be whisked out to some strange suburb to deliver leaflets for aluminium windows. They would pay us six pounds cash and that would finance more booze.

A fire burnt in a pit in the yard. We rustically gathered around the flames to tell tall tales. We toasted sliced bread on sticks. We let slip a hundred years of civilization with little regret.

There were those who dressed as punks at the weekend. There were musicians who only dressed up for the show. There were kids who lived it each and every day. Then there was us. We'd fallen down the rabbit hole; more punk than punk.

We ventured out into the real world mainly to shoplift, beg or sign for unemployment benefits. Occasionally, I slipped into the local cinema to view films like "*The Toolbox Murders*" and "*Zombie Flesh Eaters*". These were the kind of films that seldom had a West End run. They'd just miraculously turn up in some of the smaller chains with screens in the suburbs.

It is against this backdrop that I turn to tell you my strangest tale. In case you're wondering why I have been so honest about the state we were in, I need to provide a back door through which you may escape with your disbelief. Blame it on the drugs, I say. I know that I do when the fear comes upon me. I do not have the luxury of calling this fiction. It is recorded in my head not as some errant nightmare but as raw experience.

How would you spend your Halloween in an abandoned hospital for the terminally ill? You certainly wouldn't jump at the opportunity to pull out the old Ouija board, would you? You've heard the type of movies I went to see. Surely, I would know better. You really don't want to go down into that basement.

Surely, it's a really stupid plan. Even the least superstitious would write the idea off as overly creepy example of how not to push your luck and give that notion as wide a birth as was possible. Of course, they'd claim their reticence arose from the simple fact that the whole business represented a colossal waste of time but that would just be a way of covering their arses.

We, however, already lived over the Hell Mouth, so we figured we should make the most of it. If the movie of our lives was rapidly deteriorating towards the ludicrous plot twists of a B-grade slasher flick, who were we to argue. We didn't have television.

Even so, there cannot really be many folks who look at the summoning of the dead as a good idea. There was no need for a public warning. Children definitely should not play with dead things. Deep down, we knew it could only end in tears, madness and a series of increasingly theatrical murders.

Strangely, that merely bolstered our resolve. You have already seen how that boredom thing resolves itself. When you are bored, you must do something dumb because stupidity is your best defence against the tediousness of existence.

The fact that we fell into our allotted roles so easily clearly undermines the groaning and eye rolling that usually accompanies the jock kid's suggestion that we all split up because we can cover more ground. Yes, Martha. There really are kids who want to dive into the cliché. The audience may wince at the obvious plot device but someone has got to go there. No one can sit through ninety minutes of a movie where people act sensibly.

They all sat happily around the fire and nothing bad happened. The end.

Halloween comes but once a year. Determined to make a party of it, we splashed out on coal for the fire place and a few extra candles. I even bought a couple of two pence pigs trotters to hang over the fire.

We looted the high street in a shoplifting spree of such scope and audacity that the merchants of Kilburn High Road still discuss it to this very day. In the supermarket, loaves of bread sailed over the checkout courtesy of American Football style passes only to be caught and carried out the door for the touchdown. Bread doesn't cost much unless you have nothing. But ask a seasoned professional just how hard it is to half inch a loaf. It is not the kind of thing easily stuffed up your jumper. You can only look just so much pregnant without drawing suspicion.

Like good Dickensian urchins, we then hit the streets for a solid afternoon's poncing. Competition was fierce as the byways were littered with school bunking waifs anxious to corner the lucrative penny-for-the-Guy market. Begging has its limits because there is only so much loose coin to be had. We wanted it and not just because we needed to satisfy our cravings for intoxicating beverages. No, these little bastards would only go and blow their dosh on fireworks destined for the rectal passages of various small furry and otherwise harmless creatures. We had a greater duty to the pets of Britain and we were there for them, preventing cruelty through more effective begging on street corners.

We had one major advantage in this crusade and we milked it for all it was worth. Try living without water and electricity for a month and you too can take on the air of the truly fearsome and insane. It's all here in my new book: "The Beginners Guide on How to Look Like *Charlie Manson*". As you lumber towards them, people will throw money just so they don't have to deal with you. It's the human equivalent of one of those lizards that drop their tails to divert a predator.

We were scary. Even those granny mugging, drunk rolling, Queens Park Rangers supporting school dodgers would not go near us. They didn't know what they might catch but they had a fair idea. Besides, they were only QPR supporters. It wasn't like they were really scary.

It wasn't long before Bells Scotch, Strongbow Cider and a sizeable number of tins of Special Brew were on the table. We clearly did not drink for the flavour. Ruthless had somehow managed to lift a few tins of Barley Wine as a bonus. That stuff may have tasted like the concentrated piss of a Cornish leper but it sure made an ugly mush out of your higher brain functions. When you figured in the five fingered discount, the price was most definitely right. A good night was planned for all.

There was a big mirror out in one of the more neglected corners of the building. Shrouded in dust and cobwebs it dripped with atmospheric authenticity. We scrubbed it clean and in time honoured tradition wrote up the alphabet in flaming pink lipstick. Even in this time of degradation and poor personal hygiene, certain aesthetic values needed to be upheld and nothing beats Mary Quant.

We laid it out flat across the arms of a couple of commode chairs and a wine glass was pilfered from a local pub for this very purpose. This was all achieved with the kind of speed and efficiency only experience can produce.

That night the glass did not speak; it hummed. Even before the invocation, you could feel the lift under it as though the only thing preventing it from flying off and hitting the ceiling was the fact we had our fingers laid across it. It had become a living thing.

"We call out to those who hear us now, join us that we might converse through this consecrated glass. Is there anybody there?"

That last sentence is usually the laugh maker. You know how serious the circle is by how much snickering that phrase invokes. Most times, you have to say it a good few times just to settle everybody down.

That night, there were no giggles. The glass took off across the board with enough force to merit an exclamation mark. It moved fast and straight, denying the perception of human interference. It was hard to keep your finger upon it.

"Yes!"

As well as the alphabet, there were destinations for "Yes", "No" and "Bye".

There was a mutual gasp astonishment as the glass started to wear a circular groove into the mirror with its impatient prowling; a beast caged by a ring of letters. Anxious to speak, it was hard to keep up.

"What's your name?"

"S. T. V. N."

"Steven?"

It was not unusual for the glass to skip vowels. The board demanded attention. You had to keep up.

"Yes."

"Do you have a message for us?"

"D. E. T. H."

"Death? What about death?"

"D, E. T. H. C. M. 4. S. M. 1."

"Death comes for someone?

"Yes"

"Someone here?"

"Yes."

This was beginning to get a little out of hand. You could tell that some people were getting scared. This was getting a little too real. Some of us were very much into how real it was getting. You watch a horror movie because you want to be scared. I stepped up to the plate and put on an authoritarian tone.

"So, you like to scare people?"

"Yes."

"Who is going to die?"

I kind of figured it was going to point the finger at me because I had kind of gotten used to drawing the short straw. These things generally try to call your bluff when you get tough. The glass took off to the edge of the mirror closest to the young Miss America. She didn't take the news well.

"I'm sorry," I said. *"We didn't quite get that. You'll have to spell it out for us."*

"T. M. Y."

"I know you're trying to scare her but it's not going to work."

It was, however, working fairly well.

"What's you real name?"

"S. T. N."

The dropped V put a different spin on everything. No-one was thinking Steven or Stan. Everyone was thinking of the boss man. I wasn't having any of that shit. I couldn't believe that a dude with a whole infernal realm and army of the damned to run was going to take time out of his busy schedule to scare a few low lives whose souls he probably already had a lien on. Still, it's not every day that you get to argue with the big guy.

"That's not your real name. Why don't you try again?"

"R. O. S. Y."

One of the legends of Ouija is that Rosie is one of the Devil's aliases. I'm pretty sure that that little titbit also came courtesy of a Dennis Wheatley book but these were the rules we played by.

"I don't believe you. I think you're a liar."

"F. C. K. U."

"Fuck you too."

I snapped up the glass and made the dramatic gesture of throwing it into the fire place. Everything then happened at once. It was difficult to work out what were causes and what were effects.

The door to the room did not blow open. It did not blow off of its hinges. It exploded off of its frame and flew half way across the room. It was fairly impressive, accompanied as it was by a mighty roar of wind on an otherwise still night. I should mention that this was an internal door and, although it could sometimes get draughty in the hospital, we had set up camp in one of the few intact wings. Sealed ward doors protected us from the worst of the elements and unwanted intruders. At least, that had been the plan.

The wind blew out all save one of the candles. That sole survivor did, however, fall into an open drawer. The room went dark as the air filled with something that clung to the coal fire's smoke and made of itself a blacker hue than jet. There was screaming and panic. It was difficult to draw the breath necessary to find bearings. My mind didn't properly catch up until I realised the drawer was on fire. Maybe that only took half a second or so but it had been the kind of half second you could have planned your retirement around.

There was only one thing damaged in the fire and that was Tammy's passport. The front cover and half her photograph were scorched. If it had been simple coincidence, that would have been spooky enough but how many coincidences can you stack up in a pile before the ever-increasing level of implausibility brings the whole thing down?

My little old monkey brain was now kicking into gear. I naturally excluded the Ouija board as irrelevant. You can play at ghost stories all you want but, at the end of the day, that doesn't make them real.

The wild occurrences of the last minute could not have been the result of a practical joke by the night's attendees. We were all present and accounted for. Everything had happened as a result of the door so that was what needed investigating. Surely external human intervention was to blame.

I picked up a candle and a claw hammer and did the one thing you should never do in the movies. I went out by myself to check things out. Suddenly, I was the dumbass kid who was going down to the basement. I had kind of expected company but it hadn't panned out that way. The smart money was riding on cringe and huddle.

I could feel my heart thumping like it was trying to do a runner from my rib cage. The safety of the group retreated down the corridor. I felt both terrified and ridiculous. This taking up of the heroes' mantle made no sense at all.

Hey Joe, what the hell was I doing with a claw hammer in my hand?

The world had never seemed darker beyond the candle's flame. The silence made me want to talk to myself just to make some noise. Instead, I kept myself quiet because I was hunting. What was I hunting? Why didn't I just go back to the others and tell them there was nobody out there? It wouldn't be like I would have to lie.

When I turned the corner and ran into him, he appeared more shocked than I did. Standing less than a metre tall and looking like the perverted offspring of *Nosferatu* and the evil midget in *"Don't Look Now"*, he was not what I had expected. Terrified at my claw hammer wielding frame, he ran into a room and just vanished because there was nowhere else he could have escaped to. There was no other door. The second-floor windows were closed. I had encountered some sort of weird goblin motherfucker and he had dissolved into the night.

I was dumbfounded. That is such a great word but how often can you say you are truly dumbfounded? Most people say they are dumbfounded just before launching into a tirade of abuse that tends to negate their earlier claim. If I had to tell you what I was thinking, I would have to leave the next three pages blank. Rather than waste rainforests and computer memory space, we shall just assume those blank pages are there. What the actual fuck.

Morning came and, by then, the leaves had fallen from the trees, taking with them our suburban dream. The oaks and the sycamores now stood like skeletons. It was a place for the dead and we were of the living. We had been asked to leave politely and it was now time to walk away.

I only got to see the apparition once more and that was in what passed for broad daylight in November. As we left the hospital for the last time, I saw him (or it) looking down at us from a top floor window. I did not waste any effort trying to chase him down. The way I saw it, we had bucked the odds. We had walked in through the front door and walked out again. I wouldn't say we had recovered or learnt anything along the way except, perhaps, that there is some shit in life you will never understand.

We tend to record fact as though it were fiction. We tidy up the edges and impose narrative. We shuffle it around until it looks good on paper.

Unfortunately, in the real world, events occur one after another without rhyme or reason. There is no God or devil to pull the strings and that is far scarier than anything that might go bump in the night; no matter how loud the bump might be. I could try to comfort you with attempts at explanation but, really, shit just happens and life is full of little mysteries.

FOURTEEN

Figtree, New South Wales, 1974

My electric shock and near-death experience had done much to dissuade any notion of a good and loving God. I could accept that the horror of approaching death would fill one's mind with nightmare visions but, if that was some kind of portal into the afterlife, the architect could just go fuck himself.

Day to day life wasn't that great either. Childhood asthma without the safety net of Ventolin was like being in a world that constantly attempted to drown my body in the very atmosphere everyone else seemed to take for granted.

They attempted an operation to make my nasal passages larger but that did absolutely sweet fuck all.

Figtree High School housed a disproportionally large cohort of knuckle draggers determined to assert their masculinity by any cruelty available to them. Rugby League was their go to answer to most questions. It was a stacked system. If you didn't victimise others, you presented as a target.

In physical education they would make us form scrums. The opposing side would try to kick you in the guts or the nuts. Your teammates pawed at your balls and attempted to finger your anus. I'm sure there were some who considered this fun and wholesome. I'm looking at the guy with the table tennis paddle.

It seemed school existed solely to steer you into a funnel and the funnel squeezed out the human fodder towards its dedicated role. At least conscription had been removed from the list of likely possibilities. The Labor Government had kept a promise and walked away from the Vietnam War when elected. The remaining opportunities presented for us were the steelworks, the mines and the docks; industries that would vanish from the area within a decade but, at the time, were sold as our birth-right rather than our unenviable destiny.

The school loved to take us for excursions to see these career opportunities on a regular basis. These excursions were provided free by our future employers. How many times did I hear the tale of the day they spilt the molten metal and how the fleeing workers appeared to melt as they met their horrible demise?

A great piece of self-promotion, guys.

At first, I took refuge in cinema. The Regent was a mighty venue from an already forgotten time before television. Saturday afternoons were best when the venue was given over to double features that wouldn't have felt out of place in the Grindhouses of Times Square. Blaxploitation. Kung Fu. Horror movies that never provided anywhere near the gore that their titles suggested but still contained more thrills than anything that television allowed.

The room would fill with the thick blue of tobacco smoke and you could watch the image float down from projector to the screen. Then again, in those days, people smoked everywhere.

Buses. Trains. Offices. Supermarkets. Even if you didn't smoke, your clothes and hair smelled like you did.

On regular days, the Regent showed the first repeats of the big films coming off their George Street City runs. Many times, I would go to the eleven in the morning screenings and watch *Clint Eastwood* films alone in the giant auditorium.

Equally of interest to me were the old televised films; all the hits of the thirties, forties and fifties. *Bill Collins* used to show films all night on *Channel Nine*. This particularly suited my ADHD brain's utter refusal to go to sleep when it was told.

I could watch movies until five in the morning. I'd sleep for a couple of hours before going to school where I'd sit glassy eyed as some poor sod tried explaining the two times table to the numerically challenged. There was bugger all chance of academically falling behind.

My head was full of *Warner Brothers'* Gangster Movies and *Universal* Monsters. I knew all the *MGM* musicals. I could monologue all those *American International Pictures* and recognise individual Hammer Films by who was cracking the whip over the horses.

But the television was also full of foreign films (albeit poorly dubbed) from Japanese Kaiju to *Cocteau* 's "*La Belle et La Bête*" on *Channel Seven*'s Creature Feature. The *ABC* seemed to have a vault full of every British film ever made.

I think it's safe to say that, if you were alive in the Seventies, it was entirely possible for you to have seen every studio released motion picture ever produced.

But what was to truly blow my mind was popular music. I hadn't really gone in deep with modern music at that point. It was fine. I could take it or leave it. I felt no desire to go and buy a record. And, given the music I was hearing on the airways, who would be surprised?

My parent's car radio was set to *2WL* and I believe they should have been arrested for constantly driving down the middle of road. The playlist wandered through maudlin country, the most frivolous of pop with a heavy-handed sprinkling of early sixties novelty discs.

You were more likely to hear about an "*Itsy Bitsy Yellow Polka Dot Bikini*" or a *Rubber Ball* that came bouncing back to you than, say, the *Beatles*. Unless, of course, that lovely *Paul McCartney* released something as cloying as "*My Love*". They might play that but not during the Breakfast Show. "*My Love*" was a little too raunchy when old people were trying to find their teeth and eat their corn flakes.

The morning airwaves were filled with old men's funereal dirges to love. *Perry Como* drizzled the living shit out of "*For the Good Times*." *Charlie Rich* got creepy with "*The Most Beautiful girl in the World*." *Conway Twitty* terrified us with the notion that he was going to take us somewhere we'd "*Never Gone Before*". Add an overly generous pour of *Tony Orlando and Dawn* and popular music was not something you'd want to stand on in bare feet.

This was to change when, on a school excursion, the sound of Sydney's *2SM* blurted over the bus's Tannoy system. The wild desperation of *Suzi Quatro*'s "*48 Crash*" tore through the air as both revolution and revelation. This was a noise that I knew my parents would despise. And they did! It spoke to parts of my body I had not previously considered existed.

And the hits kept coming. *Bryan Ferry*'s sinister take of *Bob Dylan*'s "*Hard Rain*". The full-on assault of the *Sweet*'s "*Ballroom Blitz*". The operatic mockery of *10CC*'s "*Rubber Bullets*". The riotous outrage of *Alice Cooper*'s "*Schools Out*". The music was crass but also witty. It mocked the dreariness of the everyday.

And in this newly discovered cacophony, I found refuge from a particularly stupid planet.

FIFTEEN
Waterloo, London 1979

Campbell Buildings in Lambeth North had been a Victorian solution to chronic poverty. Build your hovels high and huddle your masses. During the war, *Hitler*'s bombs had set the tar on the roof afire. The roads became rivers of flame but the buildings stood their ground. The local tobacconist described it to me as being like an actual hell on Earth. He had probably watched it as a child. The more things change, the more they stay the same.

The initial plan was to bulldoze the estate to make way for a proposed bus and truck stop. From there, passengers and goods would be loaded onto the train to Paris via the proposed Channel Tunnel. This plan failed to materialise. Some residents had been moved onto other estates but many held out for something better. It was at this point that it became increasingly easy to open a squat in Campbell buildings.

It was almost as if someone at Lambeth Council wanted to put some pressure of the remaining residents. It was almost as if they had sent out a help wanted advert with our picture on it.

So, you want the truth about what happened? The whole truth and nothing but the truth?

Good luck with that. Writers know our weasel words and memory is not everything it's cracked up to be. There are always two sides to every story and there were hundreds of punks who spent time in those squats, each with their own monstrous egos and assorted mental health problems.

Let me just begin by saying that I may or may not have changed the names to protect both the innocent and the guilty alike. I may have combined a little bit of character A with character B by accident or design. I'll also cop to the fact that I've seen the photos and amongst all the familiar faces, I occasionally catch sight of a stranger beside me and wonder who the hell that was.

And, in a world where days often ran into each other, they may play back in shuffle mode. Memory is not lineal. Narrative is a fictional reconstruction of cause and effect narrowing our worldview to a simple yes or no. Our actions do not follow on from a single incident. We are not determined by absolutes. Our reactions are born of a giddy assault from multiple directions.

I may be an unreliable narrator but I'm doing my best with the brain cells I have left. I'm not going to straight up lie to your face but parts of the past are nebulous.

Real life is nebulous too. It lacks a defining narrative and more so when there are drugs involved. Maybe this is all true. Then again, maybe this was all a dream of sound and fury, told in a shower. If you were there, despite the blurred edges, you'd know for sure.

Or maybe not. Maybe it's better to shuffle events to better make sense of them.

No. I am being unfair to you. Rest assured, dear reader; even when I bend the facts, I am still telling the truth or at least a truth. If it didn't happen to me, it happened to someone who was like me or some other me I once was.

Admittedly, I look at my old notes and diary scraps and read words from a different country composed in a forgotten language. It is almost as if I have exorcised these demons into ink. Did I even write this? If, now, I fail to believe my own tales then why should you?

Most people write about Punk as being the history of a long list of increasingly dreary bands fighting each other over their placement in the firmament; a grand quest to be the lowest common denominator. The true story of Punk is of the urchins and waifs trying to find a place in a world they were superfluous to.

There are those who believe the Anarcho-Punk scene blossomed out of communes and housing collectives and an agenda to do good and (to be fair) much of it did. Equally it blossomed from suburban bedrooms as disenchanted youth dreamt of better worlds. But the Anarcho-Punk scene was mainly tempered out of hell on earth. For many it had to get really bad to believe in the possibility of anything better. Once you had lived in holes in the wall and endured the threats of evil men, ideas were no longer ephemeral.

SIXTEEN
Figtree, New South Wales, 1975

Musically, I suppose the next world-changer for me was the *Velvet Underground*'s *White Light, White Heat* album. It fell into my lap almost by accident. It was not the kind of music that you sought out without at least a little bit of backstory. How it affected my understanding of music was profound.

Miss Campbell was our High School science teacher and perhaps the closest thing I could grasp as cool in a startlingly uncool environment. She had the edge of that rock and roll attitude.

The class, probably seeing what I saw in her, had asked her what music she liked. She mentioned one artist; *Lou Reed*. Being proactive, I thought I'd investigate Mr *Reed*'s work. In hindsight, I imagine she was talking about the *Lou Reed* of "*Transformer*" and "*Rock and Roll Animal*". These were popular discs at the time, hanging on the edge of the mainstream. I would find myself heading further towards the left.

Lou Reed LPs sat in the rack before me in the $5.95 price bracket, far above what could be saved from pocket money and missed school lunches. At the back of the rack, for the knock-down price of $2.99 was a copy of the *Velvet Underground*'s "*White Light, White Heat*". Unlike the flimsy *RCA* pressings of his later works, the cover was thick cardboard and the vinyl weighty. Unlike Australian records of the time, it came in a paper inner sleeve. It was an alien thing with a kind of sturdy brutality. Who could guess how it got there? I immediately seized upon it. At under three bucks, the price was right.

I took it home and lay it on the family record player, a device previously reserved for the likes of *Shirley Bassey* and *Mrs Mills*. They may have had a copy of the *South Pacific* soundtrack but I think they merely indulged the phonograph as the kind of device expected in a modern household. It was rarely used.

My parents found this my new obsession a cause for horror. Without me even raising the subject, I was told *David Bowie* would not be allowed into the house. Given the stated reasoning behind the ban, it was somewhat surprising that my sister was allowed to indulge an interest in the works of *Elton John* and, later, *Queen*.

Meanwhile, as the over-cranked sounds of *Sister Ray* wrought havoc on domestic speakers, feedback had entered my life and I would not be truly satisfied until tinnitus eternally echoed that sound in my head. There was a sledge hammer of repetition and noise and I realised the rule book of good taste and somnambulist technique was not going to be playing a large role in my musical odyssey.

From there, I suppose it wasn't that hard to discover the New York music scene and the nascent Punk scene. The zenith of the alternate Australian Music at the time was *RAM* named from the abbreviation of *Rock Australia Magazine* rather than the god-awful *Paul McCartney* album.

It was actually pretty mainstream but, from brief mentions and minimalist reviews, I discovered this underbelly of pop featuring bands like the *Flaming Groovies*, the *MC5* and the *Stooges*. I couldn't hear their records but, from what I read, I liked the cut of their jib.

I kind of got excited by the idea of the *New York Dolls* along with other bands from that scene that remained little more than a whisper in the footnotes; *The Harlots of 42nd Street* and *Teenage Lust*. Were they any good? Who knows? They sounded like they'd be good.

When I saw a copy of the *Dolls* debut album in a second-hand record shop, I snapped it up for $2.75.

The guitars were the best thing I'd ever heard but I suppose it was the lyrics which changed my world. It was a realisation that lyrics didn't need to be stupid or crass. You could actually describe the world in a way that was smart but not smug. There was a sneer in the candid description of a life lived as an outcast. I felt like a sneer was perhaps the best possible response to the world.

In my mind, there was also something about the sound that reminded me of a train and this seemed exciting in a way that's hard to articulate. It sounded like moving.

The bands popular with my class mates seemed to think fussing about bustles in the fucking hedgerow made you sound intelligent and poetic. The *New York Dolls* raised a single painted-nail finger to all that bullshit.

And then we had a few glorious months where every album coming out of New York kicked the shit out of the *Status Quo* (both the band and the concept.)

2JJ had just began broadcasting out of Sydney and though it was mostly unlistenable university music, the new music occasionally crept in. You'd have to put up with the likes of *Little Feat*, *Supertramp* and *Steely Dan* for a few hours but you'd ultimately be rewarded by some *Patti Smith*. Nowhere else on the airways was giving you anything.

In 1976, I read about a live *Stooges* album called *Metallic KO* and I wanted it. Every description I read made it sound like it was the apex of a sound. Almost concurrently, I discovered someone had opened an import record shop on a side street just off of Crown Street. Import stores were a phenomenon that arose from local record companies only releasing their idea of which overseas acts would prove to be popular. Their idea of popularity emerged from the snobbery of the FM adult radio format and the desire to own yachts.

I gathered my savings but was met with initial disappointment. *Metallic KO* was on a French label and the owner had no idea how to get a copy. He did, however, have something I might be interested in. He pulled out a just arrived copy of the *Ramones'* first album.

Looking at the cover of the *New York Dolls* was one thing but I looked nothing like how the *New York Dolls* did. I wouldn't know where to begin to look like a *New York Doll*. I was three feet too tall to be a *New York Doll*. The *Ramones* looked exactly like I did.

Then the whole New York thing exploded and you'd meet a kid who had this album and another who had something else. Home taping wasn't killing music. It was the delivery system for a virus that spread like wild fire.

And it wasn't just some gelatinous dreary blob. The *Ramones* played it one way and *Television* seemed to do the exact opposite. *Blondie* were on an entirely different page again but you immediately recognised it as coming from the same place. *Patti Smith*. *Wayne County*. It wasn't so much about what it was that made it sound like a single thing. It was more like what it wasn't.

The new was everywhere and yet the new had a hidden history.

The Stooges' "*Funhouse*" and "*Raw Power*" achieved a cultural relevance unrelated to their sales. Suddenly, the first *Velvet Underground* LP was more important than *Sgt Peppers*. Or, perhaps, people were just finally coming around to the idea.

Your record collection was slapping your face and telling you that you could never go home ever again.

And then, like a bolt from outer space, the *Sex Pistols* appeared on the evening news. Within moments of the opening salvo of descending chords, high school was made redundant. Living with your parents was redundant. Every stupid rule of living your life was redundant.

The Eagles and their fucking *Hotel California* bullshit were redundant. Dickhead stand-up comedians veering between racism and the her indoors jokes were redundant. *Sid* fucking *James, Dick Emery* and *Benny Hill* were all redundant and so were cricket players doused in Old Spice and sporting ridiculous porn star moustaches.

Royal Command Performances, celebrity smiles and Saturday Night Variety shows were absolutely fucking redundant. It was time to gather up that shit and put it in the sea.

SEVENTEEN
Waterloo, London, 1980

So let me invoke actual squalor. Let me take you to the dawn of *Thatcher*'s Britain. Running hot on its heels would fall many a winter and summer of discontent. The madhouses would empty for the cause of care in the community or sleeping in alleys. There would be Poll Taxes and Value Added Taxes and a thousand other ways that the poor might feed the rich. The unions would be broken and the woman wasn't for turning.

If in doubt, take a chill pill.

Doctor Death (not his real name – pay attention) was about as bad an advertisement for five years of medical training that you could possibly imagine. Look, I'm not saying he was a bad doctor. A mediocre doctor? That's kinder.

Whilst he was assuredly mediocre in his chosen profession, that is not the point I'm trying to make here. The thing was, you'd expect some kind of reward for that much work, wouldn't you? Five years of sleepless nights on duty in a public hospital? Years of treating the great washed and unwashed alike? That had to be worth something. A little dignity, perhaps. You'd at least expect a receptionist and a car with the vaguest hope of road worthiness.

I don't know who he'd pissed off in this (or some previous) life to earn his current lot but it must have been some unbelievably evil bastard. The judge's gavel had fallen hard on Dr Manse.

Did I say Manse? I meant Death. It's getting hard to remember to change the names to protect the innocent. I have to bear in mind Doctor Death is a much more believable name for a villain and you wouldn't want me suggesting he was a victim. Just like everyone else in this story, he was forced to tread both the high and low road.

The severity of the sentence metered out to the Doctor could have only arrived courtesy of a fleet of trucks packed full of bad karma. Shit, we've all been there, done that and visited the souvenir shop. Poor old Doctor Death had also been asked to foot the bill with interest.

Condemned by the local Health Authority to work a dingy basement surgery under a Waterloo council estate in Frazier Street, he sailed ever closer to the day of his inevitable striking from the Medical Register. He had little to look forward to. There was the bottle of Sainsbury's scotch in his bottom desk drawer but that had long become more of an everyday way kind of start your day thing than something you looked forward to as a well-earned respite.

I bet retirement looked good through his blood shot eyes. All he had to do was live that long. In the meantime, from dawn to dusk, he received a steady stream of bored housewives, professional benefit recipients and punk rock zombies craving Valium and Mogadon. At least, despite appearances, they didn't want to feast upon his living brains.

Though there was that time when (name withheld but it rhymed with Fuss) chased him with a hammer whilst singing a song learnt on football terraces. *"If I had a hammer, I'd smash your fu..."* But let's ignore that unpleasant incident. If I recount each and every unpleasant incident, we'll never get to the end of the book.

As the sun went down over the Estate wall, I was not really interested in the Doctor's problems because I had enough of my own. It was a quarter past eleven on a Friday night and I was wondering whether I dared put my penis in Doctor Death's hand.

I'm sorry but I had to give you a little heads up about his medical standing and the dangers such an act might involve before I got on with the details. Standing over the toilet, inspecting the tell-tale signs of newly discovered venereal disease, it was a decision that I was not taking lightly.

There was the clap clinic at St Thomas' of course but last time I went there, the blood test had revealed a large and diverse range of pharmaceuticals. So large and diverse, in fact, that the attending nurse had loudly introduced me to all and sundry as the walking chemist shop. Such familiarity is rather inappropriate in such settings.

The doctor confirmed the nurse's diagnosis and assured me such variety of substance abuse represented something of a record in his experience. Not realising this was a bad thing, I quietly beamed at this recognition for my life's work. It was the punk rock equivalent of a knighthood. I wanted to thank the Academy.

Don't tell that to anyone. A good drug fiend has a reputation to uphold but it should be spread in whispers. Fools never rule in that School of cool.

My main problem with the staff of that venerated institution was that they liked sticking that horrible umbrella thing up the eye of your cock and giving it a good hard scraping. It is an experience that is difficult to forget. Forty years on and the wince is still there; a peripheral phantom pain on the edge of memory that causes teeth to clench at the speed of thought. If the burning sensation you experienced during urination as a result of the disease was bad, here was a procedure that would have you contemplating celibacy as a serious life option for at least several days. And in the glorious spring of youth, you have to admit that several days is a long time to consider celibacy.

The other disadvantage with the clinic was that it wouldn't be open until Monday. The sooner I got onto those antibiotics, the sooner I'd be able to fuck again. The way my dick looked, I didn't even want to touch it myself so a wank was out of the question.

I knew that I had to deal with the problem and I had a fair idea that I could just demand penicillin from the Death dude and he would oblige. His bedside manner was generally restricted to the phrase *"What do you want?"* His pen would already be quivering atop the prescription pad in bored anticipation.

"Well, I live in Campbell Buildings..."

He would write the word Valium.

He positively groaned when presented with an ailment that you didn't know how to treat yourself.

A rumour flourished about just how far a bottle of scotch would take you up the restricted substance list. Tuinal and Durophet were both alleged possibilities but, for that to happen, you would have to be able to afford a bottle of Scotch.

There were those who instinctively understood that this could be a form of investment whereby you could receive more than you gave. I was always hopeless at business.

Let's get back to the real issue at hand. The trouble would come if he suddenly decided to take his Hippocratic oath seriously. Alcoholics can be so damn unpredictable. Doctor Death could suddenly become overwhelmed with quiet sentimentality towards his patients.

Paternally, he would turn to you and tell you that he wouldn't feed his dog the crap that he was scripting out. I doubted he had a dog or at least not one that hadn't died of neglect. I figured that he sometimes just liked the company. He had once decided to stare into my inner ear for a good twelve minutes for no apparent reason other than my request for sleeping pills. Maybe he was just checking if I had any brain left in there to damage though my guess is he just nodded off.

What if he reached into that tattered plastic holdall that he carried in lieu of a black leather bag? God only knows what he kept in there. What if he pulled out some rusty hooked device of his own design? I imagined the good doctor downing another healthy swig of whisky whilst trying to work out which one of my dicks he should plunge one of his bent coat hangers into. I'm guessing that's how they used to do it in his day.

It was not a thought to inspire confidence.

My course of action was clear. Tomorrow, I had to flop out of bed before noon and see the doctor. I'd have to remember to keep one eye on the door in case he asked me to take my pants off. In the meantime, I had to take lots of downers and try to remember not to fuck anyone. Downers and fucking. That's the thing about a fistful of Waterloo F66s. Sling them in your gob and basically anything could happen in the next twelve hours.

Or not. More often than not, nothing happened. Days of nothing bled into each other, defined only by the wolves that lurked just past the line of sight.

EIGHTEEN
Figtree, New South Wales, 1976

If you opened your ears, the new sound was everywhere but it didn't sound like it came slapped out by the one big machine. Los Angeles bands like the *Runaways* and *Venus and the Razorblades* had a rather particular *Kim Fowley* chug built off of a glam rock chassis. It had a certain camp charm.

A lot of the stuff coming out of Max's Kansas City also had an overlay of camp but it felt like a more dangerous kind of camp. The *Live at CBGB's* album was essentially art rock. British compilations like *Live at the Roxy* wore amateurism as a badge of honour. And that stuff coming out of Ohio. Who knew what the fuck that was?

Add to this, there wasn't a pub band in the world that didn't want to sling their hook into any passing bandwagon. All they had to do was play those sixties soul records just a little bit faster and they could ride the coat tails of the new wave.

And, of course, Australia too would pick up bands of its own in a similar vein. In Sydney, it was *Radio Birdman* that were causing all the fuss. Not only had they access to a column inch or two in *RAM* magazine, they were also getting some play via the *"Live on the Wireless"* program on radio station *2JJ*. To top it off, they had a big in with the style setters working in Sydney Import Record shops. They were obviously gaining some traction.

Up in Brisbane, there were *the Saints* with decidedly less industry traction. Towards the end of 1976, both *Birdman* and the *Saints* announced independently produced records on sale via mail order. Suddenly *The Saints* had gotten some traction in the UK music press by ignoring Australia all together and local writer *Andrew McMillan* essentially got a leg up into the music press with his interview for *RAM*.

There was something happening and everyone except Mister Jones was getting in on it.

If you don't even have the vaguest conception of music theory, you can probably skip the next few paragraphs and not miss much. Essentially, in the sixties, a riff like the *Rolling Stones'* "*Satisfaction*" could be played on one string. Much of the *Stones* early work relied on a basic blues shuffle beat. In its root position, you play the bottom E. On the second string you alternately play a B and a C#. Smart arses might throw in a D. A passing G# was reserved for show offs. This was pretty much the basics for any *Chuck Berry* song. It was piss easy to play and everyone who did it sounded like they knew what they were doing.

It should also be mentioned that guitar amps in the early sixties were not monstrously loud and tended to weigh towards a clean treble sound. Even in the era of punk, Joe Strummer still largely kept to this sound but relied on a choppier kind of chord stylings.

But as the Sixties turned into the Seventies, the mantra of more is more grew stronger. Amps grew bigger and distortion pedals did exactly what they said on the box. The blues shuffle blasted through Marshall stacks and suddenly every pub band sounded like *Status Quo*. It was just *Chuck Berry* on steroids.

Black Sabbath dragged the 5th Chord into the spotlight. Just play the root note, the 5th and the octave of the root over three low strings and let that harmonic panzer tank loose on the opposition. Ignore blues chord progressions and the riff had come of age.

Heavy metallurgists with music degrees like *Deep Purple* would slam the root together with the 4th to create *"Smoke on the Water"* and claim they were ripping off *Bach*. Pretention is a dangerous vice.

What this ultimately meant was that bar bands could take the one note riff of *"Satisfaction"* and play the riff as a wall of sound. Simply put, riffs on multiple strings had more umph.

When Punk Rock appeared it often went even further to the extreme. Those 5th Chords could be played as 6 string bar chords (often as they were displayed in the boxes above sheet music and why would we know any better than to do exactly what was in the picture?).

Just so you know, guitars aren't really built for that kind of ill treatment. Fender Guitars and pointy-head flying Vs are a little better prepared because the strings are largely strung straight across the head. Those Gibson style square headstocks don't stand a fucking chance. That's because the G string and the D string have a really sharp angle between top nut and tuner. The D string is wound so it holds up better but that G string is heading flat faster than you can tune it.

And, just so you know, playing 6 string barre chords is fucking hard work compared to simple 5ths. But they are bloody satisfying when you are murdering a version of *Del Shannon*'s *"Runaway"* or *Nancy Sinatra*'s *"These Boots are made for Walking"*.

Listen to *the Who*'s *"Substitute"* which essentially is a sequence of three string chords played on the three thinnest strings. It has melody and shape but the *Sex Pistols*' power chord version has bollocks.

This kind of chainsaw guitar was particularly effective on the first *Saints*' album. *The Saints* also had a secret weapon in terms of *Chris Bailey*. Despite a stage presence born of drinking until falling over, *Bailey* had a wild low-life romanticism. You didn't doubt what he was feeling.

Australian *EMI* showed the kind of interest in *the Saints* you might feel when you catch the scent of a particularly rank fart. Your interest extends just so far as exiting the scene of the crime as soon as possible. Unfortunately for *EMI* Australia, the UK head office overruled them. *The Saints* promptly found themselves in Sydney playing the industry shit holes.

The old guard of established musicians really didn't want to find themselves supplanted by a new guard; particularly a new guard that sounded brutish and seemed determined to rid the world of the turgid bullshit they had been scraping their lunch money together by playing.

The satin clad Mafia lurked in the shadows like yesterday's heroes. There were various members of *Sherbet*, a band who had just plagued the world with an appalling little ditty that used cricket as some kind of metaphor for infidelity.

"Howzat? You messed around. I caught you out. Howzat?"

It was a song so vile that I still feel a strange urge to insert knitting needles in my ears on the strength of mere memory. There are those who will tell you that it went to number one and this somehow makes it a classic of Australian popular music. Ignore them. They are arseholes. In their youth, they probably wore satin pants.

As if the table could stoop no lower, they were joined by one *John Paul Young*. His crimes against humanity included that dance around your handbag classic "*Love is in the Air*". For some reason, this particular track would be taken to the heart of the gay community and prove once and for all that the pursuit of an alternate lifestyle does not automatically guarantee you the role of arbiter of good taste.

To quote *Quentin Crisp*, "The worst part of being gay in the twentieth century is all that damn disco music to which one had to listen."

Assorted lesser stars and production assistants fought over whose backside needed kissing next. It was the Last Supper as staged by *Caligula* but on a much smaller budget. The levels of fawning and simpering pushed past anything you could conceive as decadence. I swear, if I had torn off a piece of my shirt and sacrificed a single bottle of vodka, the resulting Molotov cocktail would have avenged a thousand cultural hate crimes.

Fortunately, the writing was on the wall for these pampered poodles. It was on the marquee and the posters. *The Saints* had come to town. Public assassination would have been equivalent to a mercy slaying and may have elevated these chart toppers to the status of martyrs. Besides, vodka costs money and I couldn't afford vodka. Hell, I couldn't afford beer.

I had financed this little expedition by selling a pile of useless vinyl LPs; all unwanted Christmas presents purchased by relatives who felt a peculiar need to educate me away from my cherished *New York Dolls* album. It was an odd attempt at education where the blind led the sighted into darkness. Let us test their arguments.

You like rock? You'll love "The Eagles". Man, those guys rock hard. Who could not thrill to the delights of "Supertramp"? Their lyrics are just so clever and witty. They even say "bloody" in one of their songs. How rebellious is that?

"Yes" and "Jethro Tull" are really out there on the edge playing dangerous music. I mean, the dude plays a flute, on one leg.

At the time, ideas such as these had common currency. These were home truths writ large. This was the unimpeachable dogma of pot smoking peons who craved middle class acceptance of their alleged underground lifestyle.

Bachman Turner Overdrive are a prime example of what heavy rock should sound like; tough yet melodic. Besides, unlike the bands you like, they don't look effeminate. You can really tell that Pink Floyd are genuine musicians by looking at their artwork. Double albums just drip with vision. Boston demonstrate that good song writing and classical training are the cornerstones of a successful career in the music industry.

Enough! Begone, foul discs. Get thee to a second-hand shop and bring me my sixteen dollars and forty cents. This was 1977 and - in modern day terms - that made me a millionaire. It guaranteed I'd get into Chequers. I would finally get to witness this phenomenon that had previously confined itself to a cheap monophonic record player; this thing they call the punk rock.

I skipped out of school around third period and hit the train heading up to the big smoke. Despite making my plans completely open, I had been denied parental permission.

Punk rock needs no permission from anyone.

Damocles may have forgotten his sword but he was content to squat over a powerfully large fan. I knew he'd get over his constipation at some point soon but I failed to pack a raincoat.

There are times when you just have to set sail and damn the consequence.

You may wonder why the management allowed a clearly underaged individual such as myself through the door. Let's just say that punters were a little thin on the ground at the dawn of punk. The bouncers weren't averse to throwing people in off the street. Besides, if you were paying off the cops, you needed to break some laws.

Clutching the requisite couple of bucks granted me VIP status. And I was tall so they had to look up.

Here was punk and it was beyond my wildest dreams. A fad with credibility. Simple to play and yet treated as art. And if performers could finally ditch their fucking flares in the process, that was a bonus.

The Saints stumbled on to the stage like the bunch of drunken slobs that their publican raised them to be. They had that charity shop air about them that simply reeked of bad habits. They looked like what junkies really look like as opposed to the cool rock mythology of what junkies think they look like. No, junior. Sticking that spike in your vein will not turn you into a living god. Years of drug abuse will turn you into something that looks like *Shaun Ryder* or *Shane MacGowan*.

This was not heroin chic. This was the remand wing of Long Bay Gaol. They looked exactly like they looked on their album cover. Even their clothes looked like they had been neither removed nor washed since that fateful photo session. They were so real as to be beyond real and their complete lack of anything barely resembling stage presence became a presence in itself.

Even the UK music press would desert them when they caught sight of the band in the flesh (or stood down wind of them in a bar). There was no fashion. There was no nod to style. They stood stock still and threw feedback in our faces. There was just a wall of noise and a rapidly emptying bottle of scotch.

Basically, they were simply the sound and visual of their time. I had lucked out and found myself in that perfect place at that perfect time. The offensive banality of the outside world was just blown away. I felt tectonic plates shift and empires rise and fall. I felt like *Saul* on the road to Damascus. Like a million others, I fell in love with piledriver drums and chainsaw guitar.

Back in the stalls, the old guard were not amused. The row that emanated from the stage simply wasn't cricket. It wasn't playing fair. Where were the carefully manicured harmonies and manufactured hooks? There are rules you must obey. You must pander to your manager's notion of what the public wants. If *Molly Meldrum* of the popular television show *Countdown* told you to bend over backwards, you did just that and you smiled whilst you did so.

Some of them must have wondered how they could jump on a bandwagon where the trendsetters speak a different language than you? Like irate veterans of a forgotten war, they rattled their false teeth and shook their prosthetic limbs apoplectically. They humiliated themselves with their unintended impersonations of their parents. In the face of the electric squall, their curses were impotent. Their abuse was too half hearted to mark themselves as serious contenders.

It was the end of one era and a new one had just begun. The revolution was over and the war had been won. In my youthful exuberance, I truly believed that tomorrow belonged to me. *Sherbet* would soon change their name to the even more god-awful moniker *Highway* as they attempt to follow the Little River Band into the American marketplace.

Unfortunately for them, country-tinged middle of the road required competency and, at the very least, the appearance of sincerity in order to succeed. Fortunately for us, they failed accordingly and, thus, ceased to pollute the airways with any further discharge.

Upon leaving the venue in search of Central Station, I came across a cardboard cut-out promoting something like the Greatest Hits of *Sherbet*. Don't ask me what the actual album was called. It was, however, an odd yet fitting coincidence finding these two thirds life size figures smiling falsely up at me from the gutter. A record shop had obviously found a more appropriate use for them than their continuing darkening of their doorstep. Accordingly, they had placed the board out for refuse collection. With carefree abandon, I kicked it, punched it and cast it out into the road only to see it collide with a passing police vehicle. As you can imagine, the police were none too happy. There was a screech of brakes and a slamming of doors.

After much running and fence jumping, I found myself cornered, pushed to my knees and threatened with death.

NINETEEN

Waterloo, London, 1980

Friday night. Not even John Peel on the radio. I cocooned myself in a fifth hand duvet and let the pills have their way with me. I suppose I may have thought about the choices that had led me to this place or maybe I just gave in and shut down. Pills are good at helping you shut down. Tomorrow was just one more surrender away.

We had washed up to this shore through lack of alternatives. We'd been slung out of one squat and were looking for another. The last one was haunted. The one before that had been raided by skinheads. Hunted. Despised. But surely there was somewhere we could go and build our race of atomic supermen.

Then we heard about the place where all the punks were going. It sounded like some new kind of Eden. A veritable demi paradise.

South London was always a dread option for those born North of the river and it only got worse. From Campbell Buildings, you could venture, if you dared, into streets east of Waterloo Road. Once passed the Old Vic you quickly found yourself in a long-lost decade of Pie and Eel shops. Carless streets with dirty white kids with shorts and scuffed knees threw stones and empty bottles at you. There was quite a history there.

From 1550 to 1723, the area around Disney and Mint Streets

had been outside the King's jurisdiction and debtors and wanted criminals fled there to avoid prosecution. You were said to have the *Liberty of the Mint*, though that liberty often involved being murdered or dying of malnutrition or all manner of sewage and water-based maladies. The more things change. Now we had the Liberty of Campbell Buildings.

To the south lay the Elephant and Castle shopping centre surrounded by the endless sprawl of Soviet era style estates with a burnt-out vehicle in every underground car park. Some of the pubs still had sawdust on the floor to legitimately soak up vomit. This was not some hipster thing done ironically. Here the donkey jacket ruled supreme.

We lived the low life. We were the scum of the Earth. The shat on, the spat on. The raped and abused. In Universities, they would talk about Punk in terms of a musical movement or an art movement. We were the more unpleasant reality. Whilst some played at dress ups, being a punk rocker in the squats of London was to leave civilization and enter a world of sub-Dickensian squalor; the return of the rookery. We entered the gates of the Kingdom of Abaddon and cold iron swung closed behind us.

In terms of maintaining a social order, I suppose the powers that be thought there was some advantage that Kennington Police station was a Molotov cocktails throw away. It was surely cheaper to leave us where we were rather than build a brand-new state-of-the-art prison facility. That could wait until after the new Tory Government provided suitable funding to open up the internment camps.

Another point high on the Council's agenda was that there was also the possibility (if not distinct probability) that we'd save the ratepayer's purse and demolish the place for them.

Big Ben was close, dividing the world into quarter hour intervals. A quiet inevitable passing of time. A slow burning soundtrack of suspense. Seconds pass slowly when you live in fear.

The story goes that you only get out of the East End by singing or boxing. (That particular saying is available in a number of regional variations). The squats at Waterloo were filled with aspiring actors, artists and musicians. Some had even gone so far as to acquire and learn instruments and Punk had become increasingly easy to play. The earliest Punk bands had emerged from an existing musical tradition. By 1980, many guitarists simply tuned their guitars into a major chord and played melodies up and down the neck. You could learn to play, learn a set and be stage ready in weeks.

Not that existing venues were interested in the work of urchins. Even in the recently formed world of Punk, vested interests had secured their own empires. Already the people who told you to smash down doors and burst through ceilings were reinforcing their newly won battlements.

We had always heard the streets of London were paved with gold and, out in the gutters, every bauble seemed so damn close. A veritable spectacle albeit protected by reinforced glass.

Opportunistic infections took hold. Parasites found new warm homes. Ribs made their presence felt through skin.

Down in the depths of SE1, the ambulances queued behind the dealers and that was even before people started grinding up pills and capsules and injecting them. After that, the chalk lumps quickly turned to abscesses and sometimes to gangrene.

We attempted to be a happy bunch of fun-loving scamps but generally failed miserably. We bought with us a catalogue of neuro divergence, inflicted trauma and good old-fashioned mental illnesses that could have served as a veritable library of dissertations. Moreover, we had formed a true subculture, our alienation removing us from the morals of the larger culture. Our taboos were not their taboos. Our moral compasses tilted towards a different star. It's a wonder there was not a team of anthropologists observing us.

They called her Tea and I assumed it was a Cockney rhyming slang thing based around her shop lifting prowess. The folds of a long-sleeved Westwood anarchy shirt held many handy nooks for the light-fingered. You could also soak Zoff plaster remover into the fabric for that quick glue bag hit without the stains and smell.

The real reason she was called Tea is that the girls she lived with in the squat let her stay on the condition she made the Tea. She was about fifteen and clearly admired her slightly older compatriots. If being Tea was the cross she had to bear to stand in their shadows, then so be it.

I saw her with plastic tubes in every limb inserted by doctors in a bid to drain the poison. Even if the antibiotics kicked in, they weren't sure if they could save her foot. Sickness was upon the land but – luckily – no one had thought to invent HIV quite yet.

Waking up on an unfamiliar toilet to find a strange girl from Manchester pumping some unknown chemical into your blood stream cuts through all those usual social niceties one expects by way of introduction. I don't think she told me her name but, apparently, she thought I was cute and very much wanted to go up to Waterloo Station and steal food from the railway cafeteria. My spirit was willing but my flesh urgently needed some kind of a pick me up to awaken me from my unpleasant downer induced stupor. A syringe full of what I can only assume was sulphate certainly caught my attention. My introduction to intravenous drug use thus came unexpectedly and unasked for. Don't let me try and convince you that I was complaining. I was out of my fucking gourd. Besides, it was a good lesson about not falling asleep in the toilet with the door open.

Scarecrow had been the first to die. Did any of us have real names then? Scabby *nom de punks*. Titles used to create fear, disgust or loathing. Badges that read *"Don't touch me."* Even my own name. *A bob short of a quid.* Do you get it? I just didn't have to make that shit up.

Loaded up on sleeping pills, Crow went up to the roof for reasons unknown. He might have been bored, depressed or just needed a minute to himself to watch the moon come up over the buildings. Who knows why any of us do anything? He either overdosed or fell asleep and froze. We never found out which.

By accident or design, it was a sad and lonely passing. In the morning, the police played a game where they threw tiny stones at his open mouth to see who could score the first point. Grief spilled out onto the courtyard below.

A wailing girl wrapped in sackcloth bashed at the wall with a studded belt. All else was silence. The authorities had marked out their patch with strips of chequered police tape. He belonged to them now.

From that moment on, death watched over us with an icy gaze. It was capricious but it would not be denied. Parents came to reclaim the bodies, cut and dye the hair into presentable normality and choose the suits you wouldn't be caught dead in. The dead were re-branded and re-born with long abandoned names and the promise of salvation in the arms of the Lord. Parental control, thought long lost, won out in the end. These prodigal sons and daughters found repose in the leafy suburbs and towns from whence they thought they had finally escaped. They had found their little piece of England whether they liked it or not.

The ghosts of those we knew and loved were never laid to rest. No graves marked the names we spoke. Their stories were wiped clean and altered as if Jesus was a real person and he himself had washed and forgiven them of their sins. This was a history not written by the victors but by those who paid the bills. The battles we waged looked all but lost.

Mysterious fires burst out in various flats. The arsonist in question was one we supposed our own. His name is lost to me now. I may not have even known it then. We had dragged Dirk and Lisa out of one inferno. Dirk was so out of it, he just wanted to go back to bed. He stumbled back into the burning building and, sighing, I turned to drag him out again.

Belsen was this little punk soon to be a skinhead. He was caught fucking his pet dog. We could tolerate a lot but you left animals alone. We held a kangaroo court and (perhaps believing it suitable punishment) banished him from the kingdom under threat that, if he returned, we would board him up in the toilet of an abandoned flat.

Humanity was all but dead. The world was dark and grew darker even as the days grew longer. The chill of winter eased and the wolves no longer huddled from the cold. As spring offered its first tentative touch, the darkness rose up against us in earnest.

TWENTY
Sin City, Sydney, 1977

Do you know that indentation you have at the back of your head? You know, where your vertebrae connect to your skull. Go on, reach around the back there and have a good old feel around. You know where I mean, now, don't you? I'm sure it's got some kind of scientific name but I'm not a fucking doctor and you probably aren't either. Let's just think of it as "*the spot*". That seems like a damn fine name to me.

So, you've reached around to the back of your head and you've got that spot, have you? Good. Now imagine what it feels like when there's this cold hard steel thing pressed in there. I mean the kind of thing that can put an end to everything you are and ever hoped to be. It is pushed in so hard that you can make out its shape. You know what it is without looking.

That was the rather unenviable situation that I found myself in. The cop pushed the barrel of his gun hard against the base of my skull and the fit was frighteningly snug. It was almost as if the .38 revolver had been designed specifically for that purpose. I had had better moments.

In drama, such events were common place and I was naive. I had every reason to suspect that newspapers told the truth and drama reflected the world. I had grown up with Vietnam War footage served up with television dinners; casual murders in a foreign land. At school, the Chinese revolution had been covered with a shaky clip of 8mm street executions. This whole "gun to the back of the head" thing was not a new scenario to me. I had seen it played out to its short, sharp conclusion on many a screen. Its sudden intrusion into the real world had been unexpected but strangely unsurprising. It spoke a truth about the world and its cruelties. I felt the shocking calm of those about to die. I knew what it meant to be robbed of all choice.

I didn't imagine the slam of the bullet against the back of my head. I knew just enough to know that I wouldn't feel it at all. By the time the pain hit, there would be nothing left to process the information. The only dignity I held on to was that there wasn't even time for me to piss in my pants. I considered my famous last words.

But weirdly enough, this wasn't the first time a gun had been pointed at me. It wasn't even the first time someone had fired a gun at me.

The first time someone fired a gun at me was after school taking a short cut through the bush via an uncovered road. Apparently, some inbred hick had decided I'd come too close to his property line and let loose with a round of rifle fire. The chunk that vanished out of a nearby tree was enough to convince me that this wasn't anything as benign as rock salt.

The funny thing is that I didn't even think of that as odd behaviour. This was the Nineteen Seventies. It was just something old timers did when they didn't like the look of neighbourhood kids. I don't think I ever told anyone, let alone called the police. I just remembered that, after that incident, I made sure to swing across the creek before I got anywhere near that place and detour over the other side of the hill.

And don't get me started on how many times someone had pulled a knife on me.

This, I suppose, was different. This guy had a badge. My life was in the hands of a man whose actions were askew from my every understanding of reality. Here I was; the criminal. But I couldn't imagine putting a gun to the back of somebody's head. I couldn't seriously imagine me threatening to kill another. Property? Well, that was a different matter but that is missing the point. Here was a man working so far beyond his job description that he placed me in the uncomfortable position of playing saint to his sinner.

He was a big old guy, this good man with a gun. He was just about as broad as he was tall and this bastard was tall. He looked like the kind of guy who, having formerly pursued a successful career in Rugby League, got a kick out of pulling a plough when the tractor broke down. Not that there was much call for agriculture in the rat run of alleyways between Taylor Square and the Cross, mind you. It's just my way of providing you a quick mental picture without resorting to the cliched - but true - descriptions of a neckless simian suffering terribly from knuckles scraped repeatedly on gravel.

When he spoke, he didn't speak loudly. This guy had seen one or two *Clint Eastwood* films in his time and had learnt the power of menace. He whispered, making you concentrate on his every word. Then he'd hit you with a word like 'cunt' at maximum volume with a little added spit thrown in for good measure. It left you with little doubt with regards his opinion of you.

"*Guns are dangerous things,*" he said cocking the hammer back on the gun. "*Accidents happen all the time, CUNT.*"

Well, I believed him. He had definitely made a believer out of me. Guns are fucking dangerous things. Who knew?

Hallelujah. Praise the Lord but just hold back on passing the ammunition, thanks. It was the click of the hammer as it was pulled back that had proved his point, I reckon. I felt the movement of the mechanism through the barrel and with it, the premonition of thunder and hot lead.

"*Oh shit. I'm fucked. At least I won't have school in the morning.*"

TWENTY-ONE
Waterloo, London, 1980

It was chucking out time on Friday night at local public houses across the land; the most dangerous hour of them all. The blackest of hearts were granted courage through alcohol but now they had found themselves ripped from the nurture of the bar maid's breast. Angered by these severed ties, the well-worn path between boozer and council flat were littered with half eaten and regurgitated curries, bad intentions and the bodies of unwary travellers.

We were held up in a ground floor flat. The council had boarded up the windows and we left these massive four ply sheets in place not merely through laziness but also for defensive purposes. Even sunlight was our enemy now. The only access was through the front door and, even there, precautions had been taken. Bolts, locks and chains merely offer psychological defence for those who believe their safe European homes to be their castles. In reality, these devices fail all too readily at the first hint of serious attack or police raid.

In all the flats, we removed the kitchen doors and propped them up at forty-five-degree angles against the front doorways. We propped the kitchen door under the lock whilst the other end propped neatly against the opposite foyer wall. All the flats were the same so this became a one size fits all solution. Additionally, the door could be weighted down with a mattress or heavy piece of furniture.

Those doors were all solid wood made in the days people knew how to make a door. They weren't thin plywood over cardboard like a modern interior door. They could take a licking and we often tested them to their limits. They were certified zombie proof.

This was the kind of defensive installation that allowed you to catch several winks of wary half-sleep. You just had to keep one ear open. The defensive barricade worked particularly well if it was used in conjunction with a bucket load of downers and a strategically placed blunt instrument left under your mattress. Claw hammers had become the Teddy Bear of our (de)generation.

At one point (probably directly in response to incidents I am about to describe), I converted a broom stick handle and a lamp into a functioning 240-volt cattle prod. The specific technical innovation I developed to accomplish this involved removing the ten-amp fuse plug and replacing it with an iron nail.

Though we took many chances, in our ramparts we took few. Attacks were common and we didn't take any chances by offending any deities no matter how obscure. Charms and amulets began to proliferate along with spells, talismans and hexes. We weren't fussy about which Pantheons we beseeched. We made a new voodoo from our superstitions. Certain pavement cracks were avoided whilst walking, matches were always snapped after third light and hats were kept far from beds. Various items of clothing were deemed to be lucky and were thus worn until they rotted from our skin. The line between mental illness and religion is a thin one. Once you convince another of the truth of your lunacy then all doubts are cast aside. Convince a few more and you can start picking up tax deductable donations.

It was a boy's night in and pickings were scarce. We collected our dole on Thursday and the cash had gone the way of dreams. It had vanished with the dawning. We spent the night with prescription drugs, talking and smoking Benny Hedgehogs (*Benson and Hedges* cigarettes). The floor was a gold field of abandoned packets.

There was Cory Spondence and Quick Phil, Two Tone Steve and me. Fat Phil was off sulking in the kitchen or some other dank corner. He had been pretending he was in a time warp for the last few days and this attention seeking had become rather tiresome. Cory had suggested that *Doctor Who* should get back into his *Tardis* and go fuck himself. Some of us worried he might just try that and just hoped that, when he did, it wasn't anywhere that we could see him doing it.

There were certain things you had to address when discussing life in Campbell Buildings. Self-help books addressing boundary issues were at least a decade off. Moreover, mental health issues were completely acceptable until they started appearing overtly convenient. If we had not received a diagnosis at some point, we had probably all at least fallen under suspicion.

If you started making weird screaming noises when it was your turn to make tea, this didn't help your case at all. It appeared as convenient insanity to excuse general laziness and a failure to contribute.

Fat Phil claimed his distress was related to acid flashbacks but someone who knew better said he had recently escaped from a South London mental hospital. It was probably a little bit of column A and a little bit Column B. It was, however, more likely he had just walked out the door.

If you are sectioned under the mental health act, it is very difficult to escape. Fat Phil was not going to be squeezing through any windows or hiding in a laundry basket. There was no irony in that name.

Others came and went over the course of the evening. Ruthless and Jess asked if we wanted to go to the Marquee and see *Cowboys International*. As if. There was a group who played no part in anybody's top ten thousand must-see bands list.

Pinki and Blowjob made a visit to inform us they were up to no good somewhere. It involved a group of the local estate lads and we thought it better not to know any more before the event. We'd certainly hear all about it in explicit detail later. Grossly explicit details. That went without saying.

A portable record player spun an endlessly repeating stacked loop of *Siouxsie and the Banshees* singles. After they left the charts, top forty records tended to end up in the local newsagency at forty-nine pence a pop. That put them within our price range unless, of course, the sales assistant wasn't paying too much attention. At that point, all discs were free.

I had been in better moods. Frequently. How many times could you consecutively listen to "*Playground Twist*" and still hope for a positive outcome?

The musical taste of the squats was not exactly overflowing with modernity. No-one really had the money to buy new records. What would be the point if you did? Some arsehole would half inch anything worth having faster that you could say *Notting Hill Record and Tape Exchange*.

There were a lot of pre–*Young Americans Bowie* albums having the sound scraped off their overplayed grooves. A lot of the punk kids used to be *Bowie* kids and old habits die hard.

If one recent album captured the vibe, it was *Public Image Limited's* first album. That was the soundtrack of this world. It's effortless nihilism perfectly bounced off the brickwork like a thousand lost souls.

Life was going the way life tends to go the minute some fool claims that things couldn't get any worse. The scariest thing is that people have so little imagination. Things can always get worse.

And suddenly there was a desperate flurry as someone banged on the door demanding entrance. The alarm was raised. The Scousers were coming. *Raymond Chandler* used to say that (and I paraphrase) whenever the plot started to drag, someone needs to come through the door with a gun.

Hang on a second. Forgive my ill-informed Australian upbringing but who the fuck were the Scousers and why should I suddenly be concerned about their imminent arrival?

Much like primitives who choose to live under the shadows of volcanos, we had set up home at the nexus point between a Mod pub, a Rockabilly pub and a Greaser's pub. In all fairness, the Greasers just sat around listening to *Deep Purple* albums but anyone who could do that had to be twisted in some kind of sick and evil way. One had to always quietly suspect the worst.

To top that off, skinheads were free ranging ubiquitous troublemakers. A would-be Fagin named Mad Dog ran a punk troop out of Kennington and they could also be counted upon to make unwanted intrusions. We couldn't have planned the placement of our settlement any worse if we tried.

Who were these Scousers our herald announced? Even if you religiously read *NME*, *Sounds* and *Melody Maker*, in tribal London there were hip fashion trends that passed the unhip in the blink of an eye.

A vague image formed of cleaver wielding Liverpuddlian mop tops serenading us with such ditties as "*I want to hold your hand*" whilst hacking away at various parts of our anatomy. Stranger things have been known to happen in the big city.

Of course, that aforementioned image could have been one of my weird glue sniffing flashback. Isn't there a line in the *Flaming Groovies* song "*Coming after me*" that covers this exact scenario?

There are a whole lot of theories about why people watch horror films. Some will tell you that horror films desensitise the viewer so that they may overcome their fears and learn to face the horrors life will inevitably throw their way. Others claim this desensitisation leads to sociopathic behaviour and the breakdown of society as we know it. Thus, these latter critics claim, that horror films should be banned accordingly. I think that is all a crock of shit. I believe the viewing of modern horror films provide the viewer with a range of educational insights into defensive positions suitable for just this kind of situation that had now befallen us.

Repeated views reveal all kinds of simple booby traps you can set for your adversary and which household items can be easily transformed into weaponry. That can of hairspray makes a really neat flamethrower.

The main thing you learn from a horror film is that, when you do something stupid, you tend to die fairly early on in the piece. If you do something unbelievably stupid, you will be lucky just to see out the opening scene. As is so often the case, fact proceeded to follow fiction instinctively.

Emerging from an interrupted visit to the toilet, I discovered that the front door was wide open and everyone was running to the back of the flat. The fact that there was nowhere to go back there didn't seem to be occurring to anyone at the time. As previously noted, all the windows were boarded up.

The messenger had been let through the barricades only to see them abandoned in the ensuing panic. This was turning into a frigging bloodbath without even trying.

I focussed my fear on the problem at hand. I was not really in the mood to be bashed, bludgeoned or in any way buggered. These things would not bring a perfect end to a less than perfect evening. I got the door down just in time to hear the first bangs of fists on the wood outside.

Sam Raimi couldn't have timed it better even if he tried. Actually, he did try in the first *Evil Dead* film but he couldn't have cut his timing any closer to what I'd just pulled off. Now all we needed was a soundtrack by *Goblin* and we'd have something that would put bums on cinema seats.

Amazingly, this scenario would not reach the silver screen until 2015's *Green Room*.

An undecipherable blur of drunken accents began to howl something that probably amounted to assorted threats and abuse. Scousers my arse. Drunken Irish builder's labourers more like it. Carrying enough poteen in their bellies to present a fire hazard, they lived over in the next block.

I had no idea what their beef was. Does anyone ever know what anybody else's beef is? Besides, in life threatening situations, it is often better not to know what someone's beef is. When someone is waving a sledge hammer in your general direction, it is probably better not to waste the little time you have to ponder life's little absurdities.

"Little pigs! Little Pigs! Let us come in!"

"Not by the hairs on our chinny chin chins."

Ultimately, that's about as good a translation as I can really give you. The words were all different but I think I captured the spirit of the piece. The huffing and puffing that followed seemed a little more forceful than simple exhalation. These guys were putting their shoulders into their work big time. I was putting all my weight down on the buttress and still I bounced up with every heave ho. I looked around for the nearest large heavy object.

Unfortunately, the combined weight of Cory, Quick Phil, Steve and myself would have barely matched a single sack of potatoes.

"Fat Phil! Get your fucking fat arse over here!" I demanded with the kind of voice Marine Drill Sergeants use in the movies.

Fat Phil preferred to be called Phil Free for obvious reasons. Being told to feel free seemed to demand some kind of obligation from *Mr Humphries*. No one was going there. No one was going to call him Phil Free.

There was, however, a duty to differentiate between him and Quick Phil. We called him Fat Phil because Slow Phil would have been even more insulting than our eventual choice. Besides, he was not merely big boned. He had, despite the most meagre of rations, still retained sufficient padding in order to disguise the fact that he was big boned. He wore the kind of coat that Uncle

Fester would only wear in the depths of a Siberian winter. With his thick black eye make-up, he looked like a vaguely satanic panda. Satanic Panda Phil would have made an ideal rechristening if not for the fact that it was too much of a mouthful. The important thing to remember about this Phil was that, even in a time warp, he maintained his own gravity well.

"*No,*" he replied. "*I'm scared. They'll hurt me.*"

I felt like slapping him around myself at that moment. I knew he was scared. I was scared. We were all fucking scared. My fear had bought out a cruel streak from deep inside. I went with that feeling even though he was a friend who was already close to tears. I could tell you that I spoke for the good of the group but part of me meant every word that I said.

We would all have seven shades of shit beaten out of us if the door didn't hold. Hiding in the corner would only abet our demise. If I could get him to sit on the cross door, nothing was getting through. Time to fill the breach with the nearest available not so little Dutch boy.

"*Listen to me, you fat pile of shit. If you don't get your arse over here right now, you won't have to worry about them because I will personally come over there and beat you to death myself.*"

I must have been fairly loud and fairly scary because even the banging on the front door stopped. The room took on a deathly silence as Phil assumed the position. I glared around the room.

"Now, will one of you useless fucks get me a bloody hammer so I can nail the first cunt who comes through the door."

Outside, there was a half-hearted volley of abuse and a few random kicks to the door. It was all over bar the shouting. What was planned as a simple massacre was turning into something more difficult and a waste of quality drinking time. Someone other than us might end up getting hurt. The assaulting force vanished back into the night as if they had never been there at all. The silence just swallowed them.

The next morning, when the buttress was raised, the front door was shattered and torn from its hinges. Locks and bolts hung off of bent and mangled screws but most of the damage was invisible. It lay deep within us in a place where no investigative surgery, electron microscope or endoscopy probe could find it. It was the kind of damage we all take on one hurt at a time. It's just that some of us take it harder than others.

TWENTY-TWO
Oxford Street Nick, Sydney, 1977

As you can probably guess, I didn't die. The cop kicked me in the ribs and then told me to stand up with my fingers interlocked on the top of my head. I don't know what kind of fucking gymnast they thought I was but that was harder to do than you'd give it credit. Promptly, my hands were cuffed behind my back and I was frog marched off to the paddy wagon, gun still stuck to the back of my head.

I didn't have the complete shit kicked out of me. Instead, I was merely roughed up and man handled. The occasional blow reminded me who was in charge. I was driven up to Darlinghurst lockup, just a scream away from the Funhouse.

The first place I ended up was in this room where you got to stand in your own individual wooden box. The boxes were maybe 80cms square and maybe 120cms tall. If you were Houdini, I guess you could have jumped out. I wasn't Houdini and pretty much realised that, if I tried to climb out, I'd get stuck on the lip of the box and some fucker would beat me over the head with a blunt object.

I guess they probably called it the booking room but don't quote me. There wasn't a tour guide. I just thought of it as a place I didn't particularly want to be.

There was an old indigenous guy in the next box. He gave me a few words of wisdom.

"Hey Kid. Whatever these fucks do, don't react. Don't give them fucking cunts the satisfaction."

I was a quick study. Between being shouted at in full spittle mode and threatened by un-thrown punches, I maintained a quiet calm. The shit really hit the fan when I was asked my date of birth. I watched those dull eyes attempt the maths. Numbers rolled painfully behind his eyes.

"Oh shit. This fucking cunt's underage."

The desk cop swore. *"Fuck. It's three in the morning. I don't need the fucking paperwork. Sling him in the cell and they'll sort it out in court in the morning."*

So, I got my own cell with its own wooden plank for a bed. It probably saved me from the kicking I had so rightly bought down upon myself.

Night turned to day and I got slung tea and toast. I was shoved back into a van for a quick trip to the Central Court House where I faced charges of offensive behaviour. Well, everything about me was apparently illegal now.

The Magistrate immediately noticed my date of birth. The officers who took me to the court said they had just been passed the paperwork and couldn't understand how such a mistake could have been made. I was told to attend Children's Court a week later and thrown out the door.

The school decided I must need psychiatric evaluation. Insanity or drugs were the only possible explanation for me having gone so bad, so quickly. Apparently, I had always been considered a bright student and what they saw as my fall from grace was inexplicable. I raised the issue of poor teaching methods following a curriculum that was increasingly outdated in changing times. This merely seemed to reinforce their view that I had become bad, mad and dangerous to know.

I had suggested it might be better if I were to leave Figtree High School and pursue my education elsewhere. In Ryde there was a school of film and television that basically worked as a trade school kind of deal. Sound, lighting, tape operating. That kind of thing. Instead of doing the last two years of high school, you went there and learnt the difference between a BNC and an RCA cable. This idea was immediately rejected because it wasn't considered appropriate as that kind of work was considered disreputable.

Well, it wasn't like I refused exploring options. I was at least giving them the option of *"It's not you, it's me."*

My parents had essentially ceased to notice anything about what I did. They were especially absent from my subsequent appearance in Children's Court. (Two years suspended sentence.) I had become another failure and there was still a younger child to carry on civilization as they knew it.

Did any of this bother me? Hell, no. I just needed an amplifier to plug my cheapo guitar into. All the rest of the shit could just go fuck itself.

At this point, you should realise that I'm not the hero of this story. I'm not the good guy. I'm barely the bad guy (*duh*!). I'm just riding along in the story, trying to hold on and work out where the plot is going.

You may think my disregard for my parents is a little rough. I personally just look at them as poor bastards who were also just hanging on for the ride. Just like everyone. I did have empathy for their position.

I just hadn't quite got over the time six months earlier when my father took a sudden turn and exploded into a massive rage monster. He sucker punched me in the side of the head and I had no idea it was coming. I had absolutely no idea how his internal monologue was running and how that led him to that point. In hindsight, I guess the pressure had got too much for him and he just felt he needed to hit something. I'd never seen him do it before.

I came to a couple of seconds later and I was on the floor and he was repeatedly laying the boot in.

Bizarrely, he kept on yelling that I wouldn't last two minutes in the real world. I don't know if he understood reverse psychology but I had at that very moment decided that I didn't care about the completion of high school. I was just waiting for the first opportunity to be gone.

TWENTY-THREE
Waterloo, London, 1980

And then, just as you swore things must have hit rock bottom, they found a new way to make a deep hole deeper. Darkness comes at the speed of light. Some guy called Crap arrived onto the scene out of Birmingham. He had clearly studied at the altar of Saint *Sid*.

I only said about half a dozen words to him in the time he was there because, quite frankly, he gave me the creeps by starting his conversation by demanding my spare change with what I'm sure he considered menace. Fuck, dude. Save it for the marks.

Besides, the two ten pence pieces in my pocket were already spoken for. A fifteen pence bag of chips and a four-penny pickled onion at the local chippie.

The story goes that Crap went straight up to Piccadilly Circus and hooked up with a punter. He bought the guy back to an abandoned flat in Campbell Buildings and killed and robbed him. There were rumours of hideous mutilations and a severed cock nailed to the wall. That seemed a little far-fetched to me but you know what it's like as a story passes down a line. The little details just get worse and worse.

A variety of conspiracy theories emerged but that's the way things go. Don't ever let the truth get in the way of a juicy story.

The facts were that some guy was dead and Crap fell off of the side of the building. Apparently, he was trying to climb out the top floor window and escape over the roof. If he hadn't have slipped, the body would not have been found for weeks. He'd sealed the door in the approved Campbell Buildings style; the kitchen door taken off of its hinges and wedged under the lock. Crap's spine was crushed in the fall and he then went from hospital into gaol.

But the first we all knew about it was the arrival of the Metropolitan Police the following morning. And by the arrival of the Metropolitan Police, I mean all of them. Every single one of them. They seemed to have been told to leave no stone unturned and they had been sent into a 300 flat estate occupied by drug addled punk rock cockroaches.

We all had to go up to Kennington Nick to be fingerprinted and ruled out as potential suspects. The lead detective looked like Columbo's derelict alcoholic uncle. One of the other cops told us how this guy had fallen asleep in a doorway near Tower Bridge and he'd been dragged off to the drunk tank because no-one at that Station knew him. I pickpocketed a packet of smokes of him.

Things were quiet in Campbell Buildings for a few weeks after that. There was a cop stationed twenty-four hours a day outside the murder flat. If you think we had a shit life, imagine that for a job.

TWENTY-FOUR

Figtree High School, New South Wales, 1975

I'll admit there were times when I explored the theme of evil in my attempts to navigate the world. My oddly wired brain could walk into a room and immediately recognise the complex array of relationships that were occurring. I could not, for the life of me, work out how these relationships worked in connection with me except when they involved conspiracies against me.

That's a particular skill necessary for surviving beyond kindergarten.

I did realise that my oddness made me a target for the more brutal elements. They could see I was overreactive to a feigned blow and I quickly found this overreaction led to feigned blows becoming real.

In many ways, life in Figtree High School was far more brutal than life in London punk squats. Whilst the violence in squats was more extreme, the violence of high school was gruelling, constant and casual.

I tended to just do my best to find solutions on my own. There were about three years where I couldn't read the blackboard but just found ways to get around the problem. The idea of needing glasses never occurred to me. If you were smart enough, it was easy to create work arounds.

And, in a strange way, my semi-blindness made it easier to read a room. I called it smelling the room but it was more about vocal tone and the posture and movement of people as a shape not in detail. The periphery is often more telling than the focal point.

The question *"How do you feel"* was also kind of irrelevant to me. Often, I couldn't put feelings into words. For the longest time, I thought of some feelings as huge clouds floating over me with different hues I could not explain. I learnt to express feeling through music, books and cinema. Writers expressed how they felt clearly in simple terms. I had to learn names for the clouds. I needed to learn feelings were an actual something. They were not a metaphor for something else.

A bully had spat on me from a bus much to the cheering of his friends. Apart from the obvious feeling of shame, there was a fundamental disgust for the evil that encouraged that behaviour.

Shame, disgust and guilt were concepts that I could understand quite easily. They had been drilled in to me from an early age. They were storm clouds and were not in the least bit nebulous.

I planned my revenge. I revelled in that evil and it was all so fucking easy. There was a spiral staircase marked out of bounds and it was next to the passageway that people arriving by school bus would take.

I waited in the shadows for my victim to pass. As he did, I grabbed him from behind, wrapping my arm under his chin and clamping my other arm across his face. Using my height, I lifted him off the ground and dragged him into the stairwell. There I started rag-dolling him, swaying his legs from side to side as he choked in panic.

When I finally dropped his increasingly limp form, I told him, "*Next time, I'll kill you.*"

I didn't yell this for the crowd that had gathered to observe the violence. I whispered it in his ear as though I was making a promise. The crowd parted as a walked away. I made sure not to blink and deliberately just stared into the eyes of various audience members. Especially those who had troubled me before.

It was an effective display; a grand piece of theatre (A useful tip for going on stage). He never came near me again. In fact, all bullying automatically ceased.

There are some who may take this as a lesson on how to survive in a cruel and vindictive world. I will confess there was an adrenaline rush to this act and a simple pleasure and relief in the end of victimisation.

But it did not sit well with me. I increasingly felt worse for having played the game. How could I be appalled by the evil of this world by participating in it?

TWENTY-FIVE
Waterloo Station, London, 1980

We largely foraged around Waterloo Station. There was a street market along Lower Marsh Street but we maintained legitimate relationships with the local shop keepers and stall holders. These were working class markets with deep roots within the local community. They had been surrounded by thieving scumbags all their lives and they wouldn't be falling for any of our nonsense.

Additionally, they knew where we lived and you'd have to be a fuckwit to mess with that. They all seemed to have cleavers. Even those selling undies and socks.

Waterloo Station was full of the kind of chain stores you saw at every railway station and high street throughout the UK and were staffed by the kind of people who actually didn't give a fuck. So, if you're going on a nicking spree, who are you going to call on?

So, we took up our role as part of the random vermin of the station; the rats, the pigeons and us. At the entrances we lurked between bus and train eyeing out potential coinage. We cajoled and we begged.

"Can you spare ten pence for a cup of tea?"

We did not rely on charity or liberal guilt. These were, after all, the people who had overwhelming voted Margaret Thatcher and her cadre of career criminals into office. They travelled in from their suburbs, hiding from their fellow passengers behind broadsheet newspapers off to jobs in finance, the law and the civil service.

We relied on their disgust and disdain. A tossed coin was the best way to rid us from their presence. We scarpered back to the shadows, filthy lucre in hand. The passersby scarpered in relief that we remained in their dust of their escape.

At midnight, a soup kitchen would set up under the railway arches. The bread was either stale or vaguely mouldy and occasionally both. The soup was a thin broth with occasional vegetables and unrecognisable pieces of meat served in a polystyrene cup. It could have been chicken and it could have been dog. You can actually get so hungry that you don't really care.

But at least, whoever it was who ran the van, didn't ask us to say grace or listen to a sermon about how much Jesus loved us. God didn't visit much in Waterloo and this proved he was not omnipresent. If he was, he'd have laid some serious Sodom and Gomorrah shit down on the place and we'd be first up against the wall to be reduced to a pillar of salt.

Don't get me wrong, we ate gratefully. Often, it was the only food we consumed all day. Rival youth gangs called ceasefire and huddled around blazing dustbins with the Embankment derelicts; united at the bottom of the barrel.

I found myself heading down to the station with Leah (stylised with a circle drawn around the A). In an earlier chapter, I referred to her as Tea but given the origin of that name I was fairly determined to only call her by her self-proclaimed approximation of her actual name.

By the time we had reached the station, we had already ponced enough funds to purchase teas, a ten pack of cigarettes and still have some cash to spare. The plan was then to head to the rail bar cafeteria. The modus operandi there was to grab a tray and work your way to the service till where you'd get your tea poured and pay just for the tea.

If you were, however, to wear a large coat, you could stuff a variety of sandwiches, cakes and pies surreptitiously in said coat and increase the value of your fifteen pence. This was a Campbell Building classic and, if you were not overly blatant, the cafeteria staff would always turn a blind eye.

And why wouldn't they? The food was largely diabolical British Rail fare and, at the end of the day, the huge piles of unsold items were swept up and dumped into the bin and no-one was making a list nor checking it twice. Don't ask me how I know that. Let's just leave it as desperate times calling for desperate measures and you never know what you'll find in a lucky dip.

Besides, it was all wrapped.

On this particular visit, I had been showing off, trying to steal as much as I could. I got to the counter and ordered two cups of tea that quickly arrived on the tray. Unfortunately, something else arrived on the tray. A Cornish Pasty (called the Cornish Pasty too far) tumbled out of my coat. Fortunately, I had noted its decent and, before it even hit plastic, I spotted it.

"*And, I'll have the Pasty too,*" I said confidently in a manner that suggested I really had meant to pay for it all along and I was just keeping it in my coat to keep it warm. Much to the relief of the cake and sandwiches hiding in the folds of my clothes, nothing more was said about the matter.

After lunch, Leah got on a train down towards her home in South West London. She promptly vanished for several months after being captured by the authorities and returned to a secure facility of her disliking.

TWENTY-SIX

Random observations pertaining to no particular time.

We all arrive on this rock with a hand of cards and we have to play that hand with no real understanding of the rules. In some ways, I'm probably considered fairly smart and, in other ways, I'm as dumb as a sackful of hammers. The sackful of hammers part usually leads to better stories.

I'd generally say, I got pretty lucky. I did all the dumb things and I'm still here.

Obviously, I contradict myself all of the time. There are some people whose ideas stay the same no matter what information arrives to the contrary. They are hard-wired to a single solution whilst my brain goes tripping off into any number of side quests.

There are many disadvantages to an oddly wired brain not least of which is the difficulty in forming relationships with people. Significant relationships, once formed, are focused. Small talk will never build a successful relationship. Shared trauma will form ride or die bonds.

You can also be suddenly crippled by an embarrassing memory of an utterly inconsequential moment that occurred twenty years earlier. It's kind of like *"L'espirit de l'escalier"* but, rather than a witty response, you have to put your foot in your own mouth. Your psyche can often be balanced on very thin threads but other times you are able to dismiss utter humiliations as just "*shit happens*".

There are, however, a tremendous and overwhelming number of advantages. The positives greatly outweigh the negatives.

The first big advantage is that you know for an absolute fact that you are not normal. Perfect. Who in the name of holy hell would ever want to be like them? They spend their lives with their arse cheeks firmly clamped around a razor blade fearing that any deviation from the straight and narrow is going to end up going really badly for them.

They think ADHD and autism are problems and a weakness. But these are people who have spent centuries creating slurs for anyone who doesn't fit their imagined homogeneity of mind, body, sex and soul. I prefer to think of it as a successful mutation.

I love my wild and crazy internal monologue. It allows me to get in bed, turn off the light and write a couple of chapters or an entire song before sleep finally kicks in. I love my hyperfocus that allows me to drag that monologue into the real world the next morning.

I love how a song or an idea will come into my head as I'm walking down the street or deep within a dream. Then I can pull it kicking and screaming into the light. I always believed these were things everyone could and did do and were essential to one's experience of life. But it is a gift granted the chosen few.

There is a major drawback in this. Once the fish has been landed, it is of little or no interest to me. The weight has been lifted from my brain. I have borne witness to its creation and I am relieved of it.

Normal people seem to have a superpower that allows them to shamelessly promote the mundane, the mediocre, the banal and the absolutely absurd with all the conviction of a snake oil salesman. They grow powerful on their forked tongues; casually casting pearly white lies before the most indiscriminate of swine. It is their evolutionary aberration. They have seized an unfair advantage that will ultimately destroy the species.

So why am I putting this out here? Well, clearly there must be some reason I have gone into a world outside the conventional. Sure, there is pressure from environment and society. We live in a world where bad things happen but the expected reaction is not to run towards those bad things. Clearly, there had to be a reason to take this path.

I am not going here because this happened or that happened. I'm going here because I want something. I could have got a job and kept a job. That could have solved any of these experiences I am describing. I wanted something. I needed something. I sought out those with a similar ambition even if that was simply the ambition to be something "other".

TWENTY-SEVEN
Waterloo, London, 1980

I had met Puke under rather unusual circumstances. Waking up mid-afternoon and nicotine deprived, I took a stroll through the courtyard in search of cigarettes. Campbell Buildings was an estate of five blocks of five floors a piece. Each block had six staircases leading to ten flats. Any kabalistic meaning to this eluded me.

Between each block was an expanse of concrete where you could possibly park a car. Except no-one had a car and, even if you did, you probably wouldn't want to park it there because there were all these shit cunts squatting there. And, by shit cunts, I meant us.

Calling this expanse of concrete a courtyard might perhaps create an unrealistic, romanticised version of the geography. Calling it a post-apocalyptic valley of the shadow of death may have been more accurate but I believe you'll think I'm overselling it.

I visited the local tobacconist on Baylis Road. As well as cigarettes, he stocked rows of boiled sweets in huge jars that appeared to predate the Roman Invasion. He had the morning and afternoon newspapers and a shop the size of a toilet. God only knows how he made a living. I suspected something quietly criminal. There were a surprising number of Great Train robbers who lived in the neighbourhood.

A ten pack of Benny Hedgehogs was all my pocket would bear but the day was relatively young. A little bit of the old "*spare ten pence*" and some photo opportunities with tourists would restock the coffers.

As I triumphantly struck match to box, I heard her voice from on high.

She had climbed over a third-floor stair-case balcony and threatened to throw herself upon the cold hard concrete below. In a voice that quivered with existential angst she proclaimed the world cruel and bemoaned the fact that nobody loved her. Welcome to our world.

Well, this wasn't my first night at the rodeo. I'd seen several young women hanging from those particularly rails. Pinki, trendsetter that she was, had reacted explosively to her parent's unexpected arrival. They had somehow managed to track her down and were planning to take her away. And by taking her away, I mean they weren't taking her home. They had a much funnier farm in mind.

They stood in the courtyard with what I assumed was some kind of medical professional in tow. They were yelling out one of those ridiculous names that parents think their children still answer to. In a bid to get them to leave, Pinki climbed naked over the fifth-floor rails. This particular drama had caused much excitement and bought a spectacular number of emergency vehicles on site.

We were very close to the Theatres of London's West End and such a show was too good not to get a longer run. There were variations on the theme but, if you wanted to get attention when you had none, here was a time-tested way to get it. All you had to do was climb those rails and step out over the line.

I talked Puke down fairly easily. A fall from the third-floor balcony was going to result in broken limbs at worse and hanging on for an extended period was tiring. Besides, she had got someone's attention.

We sat on the wall overlooking the road and I broke out the cigarettes. We watched the afternoon traffic as it drearily crawled off towards the south-west. Kennington, the Oval, Brixton and then all the way down that long crawl to Croydon.

We kissed and she told me that, if I didn't fuck her, she would climb back out onto the balcony. Well, who was I to argue with that logic? I was a young man with all bits working. I had no desire to watch her hanging off the balcony again.

As Jarvis Cocker had noted, "*I said I'd see what I could do*". It all made a quiet kind of sense at the time. Who says gallantry and the age of romance is dead?

A couple of hours later, she had scarpered. She thought her boyfriend would probably be worried. Puke strapped on her Doc Martins and headed back to the wilds of Kennington. Oops. She was part of Mad Dog's crew. Any contact with that lot always ended badly.

Later on, it was suggested by someone that she looked like she was fourteen. That clearly wasn't true but the possibility, once spoken, suddenly became a concern. Maybe that was true. There had been a biting sarcasm attached to the suggestion. But what if it was true?

Seriously. If I thought that was true, would I write it down? But doubt is the question here. Let's follow that.

Was this the real meaning of the liberty of Campbell Buildings? Were we merely living in a world where we could justify any bad behaviour by ignoring exterior morality? A land of do what you want. If that was true, what separated us from the thugs and bullies? Did claims of being beyond good and evil mean we were without sin?

If you were living in the squats, you were a grown up escaping your parent's and society's clutches but that did not make us saints. We could still find ways to hurt and belittle each other. Was it jealousy or just another little stirring of the pot for entertainment. Boredom was a factor. Cruelty, rumours and lies were not uncommon.

With such a large group of reprobates gathered in such close quarters and with so little to do between ponced cigarettes, gossip was the order of the day. Cliques, sub cliques and secret societies blossomed. There is power pulling the wings off of flies.

But this amorous encounter had indeed bought the Gods' displeasure down upon me. I found myself surprised to find I had acquired some new friends during my latest adventure.

"*What the hell is that?*" I asked as I took note of some peculiar lumps attached to the roots of my pubes.

Plucking one abnormal hair, I lifted it to the light.

"*What is that thing? It looks like a tiny crab.*"

And with a single word, revelation came. Soon I would visit St Thomas'. The doctor would decide I could probably do with a full check. Oh. I've told you that story already.

TWENTY-EIGHT

Canberra, Australian Capital Territory, 1977

In Sydney, the band to see was *Radio Birdman*. They had the magic. Equal parts serious and fun. Razor sharp eyes for the cool on the edge of culture. And, best of all, you bought your dancing shoes. It was the hot ticket.

They'd basically set up clubhouse above the Oxford Tavern on Taylor Square; calling it the Funhouse in tribute the Stooges second album. This was the flame the moths were drawn to. The place where all the kids meet. The PA picked up the sound of passing taxi radios. When the band played the sprung hardboard floor literally bounced with the excitement of it all, going up and down two or three inches with every snare beat.

And, when the band played somewhere else, we happily went to where ever it was they were playing without any thought of where we would stay or how we were getting home.

We were never going home anymore.

This was a moment in time when you had to be there regardless of any consequence. Every night made history.

It was early in August and I caught a train to Sydney at sparrow's fart to catch another train to Canberra. Fortunately, there were a lot of familiar faces aboard the train; a fair chunk of the Funhouse crew.

Unlike many outings by groups of young people, this was a pretty sober affair. No-one was getting wasted on the journey, it was good natured comradery. We just talked about shit which was something you really didn't get to do in the environment of a punk rock gig. Screaming feedback tends to make conversation difficult.

The important thing was going to see the band. The band was more exciting than getting drunk or getting high. The band was what you had waited for throughout the dreary days of High School.

Birdman were playing the first night of this micro tour at the University and benefitted enormously from the big stage. With the *Hellcats* as support, they pretty much smashed it. Well, the gang all thought so. The locals were pretty much shell shocked. It wasn't that they disliked it. It was more just the shock and awe. The gulf between Punk and the Rock that came before was as huge as night to day.

In Sydney in winter, when you say it's cold, you put on a light jacket and you are hot. The Pacific Ocean basically keeps the worst of it away. It would be an unlikely day that it snowed in Bondi. With only two hundred and fifty years of recorded history, I can't say it could never happen but you get the picture.

As we left the University building, it was properly cold.

Canberra is about 300km south of Sydney and 150km from the coast. It has an elevation of 600m. When I say it gets properly cold, it gets properly cold. Testicle shrinking, face frozen, dead in a doorway cold. They have things called the Snowy Mountains just down the road.

Come closing time at the Funhouse, the publican would wander through the room demanding we do our talking out on the street. I'd been talking outside with Kath and Jodie when suddenly we realised that everyone else had fucked off. This was almost certainly because it was so fucking cold.

We were just the dumb fucks who got carried away, talking about how exciting the night had been. It was dark and quiet and we finally got it through our thick skulls that if we didn't start moving, we were going to die.

Canberra was not heavy on night life and seemed to have more than its fair share of nothing. There wasn't even a light over at the Frankenstein place. Finding shelter seemed about as likely as finding a street light. As the nation's capital, it made a fine arctic tundra. Denim gave no protection from the wind. The dampness was quietly turning into ice.

We trudged through the darkness, forcing step after step. We trudged without hope; without plan. You know, the kind of trek you have to make in a book before you obtain revelation.

Finally, we spotted a youth hostel and hoped we had enough cash. The front door was locked but we were desperate by that time. Fortunately, we found an unlocked side door and slipped into a reception area. There wasn't anyone at the desk and only the most minimal of lighting shone down the corridors.

What it did have was central heating and some benches. We had reached the end of all endurance. We thudded down like heaps of human refuse and were asleep in seconds.

At about six-thirty, the day shift rolled in and promptly chucked us out into the street. It didn't matter. The sun was coming up, the morning frost retreated and we had survived the night. We went off and found a park and slept into the afternoon.

Weeks later, I would lose my virginity with Jodie. Years later, I heard she died after injecting drugs cut with bleach.

TWENTY-NINE
Waterloo, London, 1980

I had gone to London with the simple plan to form a band and play. With all the punks hanging around the squats, it hadn't been difficult to enlist band members. Everyone wanted to be in a band and, I've got to be honest, it's not that difficult to pick up the rudiments of instruments.

Have you spoken to a musician? They are only, very rarely, rocket scientists. It's like driving a car. You might make a huge fuss about how difficult it is getting your licence but it's not like there's any limitation based on a low IQ.

Punk and Rock largely come from having an idea and working out a way to present that music. Many people talk of technical ability but the last thing you want to do is get up on stage and concentrate on what you have to do. You look better thrashing out one mighty E chord than you do hunched over a twiddley lick. If you have to watch your hands, you are doing it wrong.

Essentially, living unemployed, we also had time to rehearse even if that was through no amps and pots and pans drums. We had enough general knowledge of a set that the odd trip to a rehearsal studio kept us game fit.

Getting to play a gig was another thing altogether. For a start, referencing Karl Marx, we didn't own the means of production. The venues were largely set up as a club to protect the existing industry. The dedicated punk venues were largely gone by this time. There was no Roxy or Vortex.

Some smaller scenes had developed their own venues but they were vested in their own interests. The sons (and occasionally daughters) of *Garry Bushell* had their bald-headed thing going out in Canning Town.

Agencies largely acted as gatekeepers to established venues. To break in, you needed press and to get press you had to play. It was that or give out really unenthusiastic hand jobs.

Another big problem was that we had no fixed abode. We'd squat a flat in Campbell Buildings and two months later we'd be chucked out only to move into another. We weren't getting any return mail anytime soon.

As for this new invention called the telephone. Well, we knew they existed. It's just ours was in a red box out on the corner of the street and it wasn't taking incoming calls. Poverty is a one-way trip back to the stone age.

Someone had run into *Cowboy Jock McDonald* at Billy's Club in Dean Street. He said we could support the *4" be 2"s* at a pub just off Camberwell Green. When we arrived with most of the Campbell Buildings punks in tow, we were removed with extreme prejudice. Even the bottom of the barrel didn't want us around.

Alaska Studios, under the arches at Waterloo Station offered a deal where they'd record a demo for fifty quid. We recorded two songs but the staff couldn't deal with us so they chucked us out and said they'd mix it for us. We were so stupid that we thought that this was how it was done.

The result was so fucking awful that I believe Lisa destroyed it, pretending it was stolen. I know I couldn't listen through it.

It was a Friday night and Lisa and I had decided we would try to write a song together. We had a couple of jars of pills, vodka and a guitar. It had been quite successful. We'd already knocked out a song called "Roles" and we were well underway on one called "Tomorrow".

We literally heard their arrival from a block away. As I said, the courtyard outside Campbell Buildings didn't see a whole lot of vehicular traffic. Occasionally, there would be the tell-tale hum of a black cab's diesel engine. This noise, however, was the heavy-handed arrival of multiple police vehicles.

The big give away was the chatter of their radios which you could hear even before they opened their van doors. Charlie Uniform November Tango squawks filled the cold night air. All illicit substances vanished long before their jack boots hit stairs.

Of course, the cops weren't that worried about making arrests. This was just the common or garden harassment they liked to dish out just to remind us that this was their world and we only lived here.

Don't be silly. Of course they didn't have a warrant. All they had to say was that a person dressed like a punk rocker had committed a crime and was seen entering the estate. They were in pursuit of a suspect. Given the squatter's lifestyle, they probably weren't even lying.

This bunch of mouth breathers were about as bright as they come. Even though every light in the place was on, they still wandered around with their torches on. We ignored them as they casually uplifted chairs and furniture and smirked stupid questions. We'd swallowed a shit ton of Valium. Half an hour from now we'd still be on the mattress. The main difference would be that we soon would be snoring.

They, on the other hand, should have been wearing rubber gloves. Who knows what they might have caught off of the soft fabrics.

One morning a bunch of about eight of us all got up and decided to go somewhere. I can't remember where we were going but it might have been the Tate Gallery because we were heading West along Upper Marsh Street. And we all had a genuine interest in modern art.

The cops jumped us under the rail bridge and said they were going to arrest us because we were drunk and disorderly. God damn. It was about eleven o'clock in the fucking morning and we hadn't even had a chance to get drunk.

We had, however, stolen some bottles from an off license across

Westminster Bridge Road but they didn't know that and we hadn't even had a chance to open the god damn bottles. So, getting arrested for being drunk was fucking absurd.

We were about to spend the rest of the day in the cells. In the back seat of the car, Lisa had slipped me a few Tuinal so I did not give a fuck. It was hard work swallowing without water but, sure as shit, I was out for the next sixteen hours.

The next day, we went to court and were sentenced to a day in gaol. We were released because of time served and they gave us back the shoplifted booze.

THIRTY

The Illawarra Line, New South Wales, 1977

A little-known benefit of being in a New South Wales high school in 1977 was that when you passed the age of 14 years and 9 months you were entitled to a rail travel card. This enabled you to buy any train ticket for fifty cents. You picked it up from the office at school but it wasn't publicised and it really wasn't common knowledge.

What it meant for me was a return ticket from Wollongong to Sydney was fifty cents. And with that little piece of cardboard, I had my freedom. If I wanted to go record shopping at White Light. If I wanted to go to the Funhouse. No problem.

According to the fine print, all I had to do was remember not to fold, spindle or mutilate.

Riding the train came with its own sets of adventures. It also had its bonus set of misadventures. Unlike modern public transport, you were stuck in a box where there was a fair chance of interaction with your fellow passengers. In a time before mobile phones and entertainment devices, there were bored people on board. And bored people are statistically the most dangerous of people. Then there were the crazy people and they were easily bored too, particularly when they weren't doing something unspeakable.

On the last train out of Sydney on a Friday night, you had every chance of meeting the very drunk, the very stoned and the absolutely fucking insane.

Additionally, the infrastructure was not always in good repair. There were many times the train would just judder to an inexplicable halt. There was no public address system and, at times like these, the guard and the driver knew better than to mix with the hoi polloi.

One night, the train died just near the platform at Helensburgh Station. It sat there for four hours. I've felt safer in prison cells. I've felt safer with bears in the woods

A *Radio Birdman* badge was a good introduction because there was a fair bit of traffic to and from the Funhouse. I met a guy in a band called the *N-Lets*. They were going to Wollongong University and I was impressed they had a song called "*Do the Granville*", named for a recent rail disaster.

I, of course, had my own obsession with the idea of songs about dancing, though "*Do the Harold Holt*" was little more than a title at the time with a dance attached vaguely reminiscent of "*The Swim*" from the sixties. Harold Holt was an Australian Prime Minister who went for a swim one morning and was never seen again. Many years after the song, to do a Harold Holt became rhyming slang for doing a bolt (or running away).

I'd meet lots of kids going off to see bands and wanting to be in bands. Their taste generally ran a little too straight for my liking but, you know, there's a commonality there too. A dream to live outside the lawnmower hum of working-class suburbia. A place where loud guitars and drums represented a kind of freedom.

Heading up to the Smoke on a Friday evening you'd always find creepy Christians getting on at the Shire. Sometimes they'd send girls over to flirt with you and they'd say you could go back to the church with them and there were beds and you could stay there. It was dead eyed zombie land, pimping for Jesus. They'd always deliver their schtick like they were going to bury you in a shallow grave.

Of course, creepier things happened. One night, this big guy in his late twenties starts talking with me. He looked like a hippy rugby league player. We were just talking like normal shit and I was not getting any weird vibes at all. Thinking he looked like a rugby league player was probably a warning sign bubbling up from my sub-conscious.

It was one of those carriages where the seats are grouped in a pattern of four facing each other. Suddenly he's across the chair, trying to stick his tongue down my throat. This guy is strong and he's got weight and I'm pretty much stuck under him. My major concern is keeping my lips clenched and his tongue anywhere except in my mouth.

He finally gets off me and it's only then I realise the bastard had come all over my jeans. But this was not the creepiest thing.

"I hope you don't think that I'm some kind of a poofter," he said as he returned to his seat and readjusted his pants.

Given the circumstances, I considered this one of the wackier statements I'd ever heard. I sat there in a state of shock until he finally got off the train.

You might think I'd stop catching the trains after that. No chance. No matter what the world threw at me, I wasn't giving away my freedom.

THIRTY-ONE
Waterloo, London, 1980

Demolition had already begun on the most Easterly block and various stairwells of the second had been sealed. Cyclone fencing marked off the demolition no go zone. The nights were growing longer as the Winter began to make its presence felt.

I was alone in one of the flats on a Monday night. Mondays were usually quiet but everyone seemed to have gone off somewhere. Overall, there was the overwhelming air of rats preparing to flee a sinking ship.

There were unfamiliar voices on the stairs reeking malice of forethought. I had a gut reaction. It was some of the Kennington punks out seeking trouble. That's right. I told you there was going to be trouble. Some predictions take root in your bones and essentially become unescapable.

They banged on the door. They kicked on the door. They huffed and they puffed and they blew at the door. They screamed threats of murder and that certainly didn't encourage me to let them in.

Obviously, I had wedged the kitchen door in place. I dragged a mattress onto the kitchen door and I lay across the mattress and thought to myself, "*Not by the hair of my chinny, chin, chin, motherfuckers*".

They kicked and dived and punched at the door seemingly doing more damage to themselves than the barricade. This continued for a good half an hour. They were being particularly determined little fuckwits.

One of them then got the idea of putting paper through the letter box and setting it on fire. This escalation was easily dealt with thanks to a pot full of cold water.

The big bad wolves then threatened to pour petrol into the mailbox and burn me alive if I didn't let them in. Firstly, letting them in so they could murder me wasn't really going to work for me. Secondly, I figured that, if they did have petrol, we wouldn't be having this conversation.

Still, I considered my options. I could open a window looking out on the rear court yard. I was on the first floor so, if I grabbed hold of the sill, I could lower myself down. The final drop would have been less than two metres. That was doable. I might even be able to throw a mattress out ahead of me to help break the fall.

A strange calm came over me. I was going to be okay no matter what these numb nuts did. It almost became funny. The storm raged at the door with impotent fury and all I needed to do was hold my ground. Eventually, they just pissed off back into the night.

The end for the squats of Campbell Buildings came swiftly thereafter. A couple of days later, a cop got stabbed to death outside of Boots on Lower Marsh Street. From what I heard, this creep had added a few items to one of Doctor Death's prescriptions. The forgery was pathetic and the pharmacist called the cops. There was a struggle outside and, in an act of stupidity, the guy pulled a knife. He was one of Mad Dog's crew; maybe even one of those arseholes who had recently paid me a late-night visit.

The trouble was, he was a punk and the staff of Kennington Police Station told us someone had to pay and that payback would be a bitch. We took the hint and moved on.

Now, I've pretty much been avoiding any moral high ground. Essentially, I've been sticking to reporting the facts or, at least, the facts as I saw them. There is no good reason to kill someone because you want drugs.

However, living in a world where you are so desperate for drugs that you are ready to kill for them isn't really that great a thing either. Prohibition has always been society's way of punishing and criminalising the most vulnerable.

Drug use is not the great failing of individuals. It is the failure of society to deal with the trauma, disengagement and despair of individuals. Addiction should not be a criminal issue and, whilst it can be a health issue, the central problem is how the society operates against those who cannot fit within its boundaries.

THIRTY-TWO
Ashfield, Sydney, 1977

What is the worst name for a punk rock band ever? A lot of them were just generic shelf picks with every available letter A circled. Bodily waste provided a few shockers. Quite a few just dripped with toxic masculinity as if it was a badge of honour. Others just tried to humorously offend like *"The Turd Burglars"*.

Sydney in 1977 had a few stinkers largely based on what appeared half hearted disinterest. Bands like *"Tommy and the Dipsticks"* and *"Johnny Dole and the Scabs"* seemed to live off of what, at best, were place holder names.

My nomination for the worst name is *"West Coast Live"*. It was not an offensive name as such nor was it a particularly stupid name. It was just incredibly ill considered. It evoked images of *"The Eagles"* and all that drizzling shit that *2JJ* would call adult orientated.

Placed in the context of punk in Sydney in 1977, it was downright ludicrous. What did it say about the band? What did it mean? It was too absurd to even pass itself off as irony.

We are on the god damn east coast.

When *West Coast Live* got the *Psycho Surgeons* to support them at Ashfield Town Hall, they must have been asking to die. The *Psycho Surgeons* were not the most popular of bands to emerge from the Funhouse scene. They were, however, the most shambolic and authentic. If you've ever heard an *Iggy and the Stooges* bootleg during their post *"Raw Power"* death trip tour of America phase, the *Psycho Surgeons* could have easily played support.

Theirs was the sound of magma poured over surf beat drums. They were a band who always played under an unshakable dark cloud. I think they were my favourite band on Earth.

The Funhouse had ended with a bang and not a whimper. Whilst *Birdman* and the *Hellcats* were off playing in Canberra, Paul Gearside, the singer with the *Psycho Surgeons*, had been living the dream of doing all things *Iggy*. A gang of Bikies had obliged by helping him re-enact the *Stooges'* last stand upon his wedding tackle. Finally, East Sydney really was the Michigan Palace and broken teeth tumbled out of split bloody lips. If someone thought of rolling out that old chestnut about being careful what you wish for, history failed to record it and we most certainly failed to pay it any heed.

At Ashfield, the *Surgeons* stumbled through their set to little or no reaction from, what was then, a suburban audience. (Today's Sydney siders would be confused to think of Ashfield as suburbia but many years have passed since then). A few of us Inner City types were up the front cheering but mostly the local lads were sucking back piss and throwing up at the back of the hall.

Within the first three songs, *West Coast Live* had managed to play *Jean Genie* and *Suffragette City*. Singer, Pete Tillman, had already tried to do that stupid *Lindsay Kemp* mime thing with the invisible wall and the empty cans were raining down. (When the *Boys Next Door AKA the Birthday Party* first came up from Melbourne, *Nick Cave* did the same thing to a very similar reaction). By their next *Bowie* cover, which didn't take long to materialise, a lot of people had decided that heavier objects would perhaps do a better job of clearing the stage. *David Bowie* was not popular with the suburban crowd who were rather suspect of the whole make-up thing. *West Coast Live* were going down. Pete Tillman could have that effect on an audience.

Look, it wasn't that they were that bad a band. They were just kids playing covers of the things they liked. How were they to know that many of us upfront had different gripes with *Bowie*. Many had cheered Ron Hellcat on as he stood on the Funhouse stage and smashed his copy of *Ziggy Stardust* in retaliation for *Bowie*'s production of *Iggy*'s "*The Idiot*". For us, *Bowie* was too straight.

Essentially, *West Coast Live* were being shot by both sides.

These days a band like *West Coast Live* would have gone over a bomb at the Moshpit or maybe even the Marrickville Bowlo. If they had decided to play their 1977 debut in Melbourne, they would have probably had their collective cocks sucked by every boy and girl in the room. *West Coast Live* just picked the wrong audience to play to at the worst possible time in human history. Being a covers band was bad enough but getting one of the original Sydney punk bands to support you was simply asking for trouble. When our bands went out into the sticks, they were canned and booed and beaten. Payback was just a frigging bitch as we took it out on these old school pretenders.

And let us not forget that their name sucked.

When Matt Dickson of the fanzine "*Self Abuse*" asked me what I thought about *West Coast Live* and their singer, I launched into a lengthy diatribe that included an eloquent comparison to the life work off the Egyptian Dung Beetle. I wouldn't like to say exactly what this comparison entailed but it was extremely crude and humorous in nature. There were some at the table who wept with laughter as I ventured this opinion.

Unfortunately, Pete Tillman is now a highly paid and well-respected lawyer and it would probably be wise not to slander him.

Matt told me that Pete would be the first to agree with everything I had said. I doubted that. I felt the singer's self-opinion probably lacked the same kind of brutal vulgarity and personal defamation that I had brought to the table.

I was told Pete thought his band stank, the material stank and he wanted to play in a band like the *Psycho Surgeons*. Nobody else seemed to want to play in a band that sounded like that except me. It was clear to Matt that I should form a band with Pete not based on any talent but on common ground.

I thought about this for a moment. One of the first rules I developed through my neuro divergence was a simple one. Your first opinion of someone is always right. Later on, they may twist you around their finger with their cold calculated normal brains but the truth of it would always come out. First opinion was always right.

"*Sure*," I said. "*Why the fuck not?*"

Here was a singer who seemed to have the ability to inflame an audience to mindless violence with just one single syllable delivered via phoney American accent. Everyone was going to hate us because they were going to despise him. That sounded so much cooler than being loved.

THIRTY-THREE
London, 1980

The initial idea was that the band wouldn't have a name at all and this is what would separate us from other bands. We would have a symbol largely based on a hammer and sickle with the hammer stylised to suggest a swastika and the sickle suggesting a question mark. It was an arthouse move and would prove unworkable but it formed the basis of a vision. And you should have a vision even if that vision is idiotic.

We were punks. We looked more punk rock than any punk rock band. We lived in punk rock squats. And, God damn it, I'm pretty sure we must have smelled like punk rock but we probably had all become acclimatised to that particular foul odour.

That didn't mean we particularly wanted to sound like one of all the other punk rock clone bands around us. We'd all been around long enough to know what punk sounded like before it found a uniform. There was also enough off-centre stuff emerging in what would be called post punk to suggest there were other ways of doing business.

We wanted to keep the energy and fury. We could handle the Dolls/Pistols structure really well. We figured we keep some of that and fill the set out with weirder, noisier stuff. I retained a particular love for feedback because it was like riding a wild horse. You could never totally bend it to your will. All bands steal ideas but we went out of our way to not steal everything off the same shelf.

I had songs. I had a shit ton of songs. Some I had dragged from band to band like chewing gum on my shoe. Some of them I can still rattle off on stage every now and then.

We played a party in a huge squat in Holborn. The line-up of the band was still a little loose but I remember we played a pretty wonderful version of Louie Louie to round off the night. After the gig, one of the Slits jumped on my back and shoved her tongue in my ear. I considered that to be a successful outcome.

Eventually, the band became Lisa on vocals, Ruthless on bass, Richard Morgan on drums and me on guitar. Sometimes, we rehearsed in a basement in Islington. Listening back to cassette recordings of these recordings was not something that everyone could enjoy. We could certainly clear a tube carriage by hitting play on the cassette.

The thing was, the sound was there; even in the rough and tumble of a condenser microphone. And like a million other kids who had ever picked up musical instruments before us, we had wrestled something out of the aether that would not have existed without us. We felt like Gods.

Dirty, smelly Gods.

THIRTY-FOUR
Sydney, 1977

We met up at McDonalds on George Street. Not only was it a central location, it also had the advantage that Dave Tozer worked behind the counter. He clung to the periphery of the early punk scene and, to this day, he plays in a band called *The Overtones*. He also provided us with sly upgrades on our orders. Small would arrive Large. A cheeseburger would arrive as a Big Mac.

Back then, McDonalds had coffee spoons that apparently were perfect for snorting coke. None of us could afford coke so, outside of dreams of avarice, we couldn't tell you for sure.

You could still smoke at the tables back then. Any table. In fact, you could lean over the counter with a cigarette hanging out of your mouth, blow your exhaled smoke over all the food and no-one said a damn thing.

The disposable tin foil ashtrays were piled high with the debris of cancers yet to come left by an army of previous diners. Through the nicotine haze, our fellow patrons looked at us with an outraged disgust that it is hard to imagine in these more liberal times. A blue haired biddy at the next table shielded her grandchild's eyes and told him not to look at creatures like us. I figured she (or someone she loved) must have fought in the war for people like us and now felt she had picked the wrong side all along. For her, killing Nazis meant she had ended up with the bad end of the deal.

We weren't actually doing anything. We weren't spitting, drinking, swearing or being particularly rowdy. And even though you could smoke, none of us did. We just didn't smoke.

We did, however, seem to dirty the place up in the way that only young men can. We had bad posture and worse haircuts. Our very presence infuriated this woman beyond human reasoning.

We continued discussing what we should call our brand-new band.

The woman grew apoplectic. She angrily flicked ash at the floor, stubbed her cigarettes into her plastic McDonalds tray before chaining the next one. Finally, it had all gone too far and she exploded.

"You're Filth! You're nothing but Filth," she bellowed with no sense of irony.

What could I say? She had absolutely fucking nailed it. I bet she hadn't even seen the recent screenings of *John Waters'* *"Pink Flamingos"* at the Paris Theatre.

Calling the band *Filth*? What a perfect alignment of form and idea. Feeling the need to celebrate theatrically, I opened my shirt and safety pinned an ash tray into the top layer of skin on my chest as if it were a medal. Exit woman screaming, leaving nothing but a half-eaten meal and our new band's epitaph in her wake.

How could we live up to such a moniker? Well, we sure as hell would try.

One idea was that we should be a punk band in the absolute sense of what straight media said about punk. We would be tuneless and talentless. It was simultaneously an art school prank and, because none of us had actually gone to art school, it would be absolutely and one hundred percent straight faced and serious.

Pete sang. Elvio, another refugee from *West Coast Live* played bass. He preferred to be called Elvis (as you would). I played guitar and wrote the songs. I made sure that I always had a live microphone on stage but not because of any desire to sing backing vocals. Instead, I needed something to abuse the audience through and talk stupid shit. Because we were truly awful, it was hard to find a drummer. We got anyone we could to fill in that empty chair.

We practised with unplugged electric guitars because we didn't have amps. Besides, we thought that if we could make that sound good, we would sound even better plugged in. Have you ever just bashed the living shit out of an acoustic guitar hitting all the strings at once? Sounds fucking awesome, doesn't it? Besides, I was always fairly certain that guitar playing was somewhat over rated. Most records you heard, the bass was doing all the work melody wise. The guitars (apart from the fiddly bits) and drums were usually so low in the mix that you could barely hear them.

The idea that this strategy would produce any kind of commercially viable music evaporated about twelve seconds into our debut performance in Lismore. But the noise we made wasn't just awful. It was confrontational and surprisingly funny. No matter how badly we played, our natural buffoonery seemed to entertain and horrify in equal measure. We had, through accident and not design, somehow created something that had not walked the Earth before.

Instead of guitar solos, I decided on breaks of screaming noise like the *Velvet Underground*'s *Sister Ray*. If you are thrashing away on all six strings and you move into single note solos, it sounded like a massive drop in energy. And besides, there was no way any of the strings were going to be in tune after the hammering I had given them. Instead, I ran my left hand up and down the guitar's next, randomly hitting any note without mind of key or harmonics.

Song structures generally ran verse, chorus, verse, chorus, noise, chorus, chorus, feedback. We couldn't find a drummer who understood the noise bit until we found Noel.

Noel couldn't drum at all. He was like a primary school percussionist on very bad drugs. Actually, he was famously on bad drugs all the time and smack allowed him to vomit at will. Come to think of it, there was actually nothing about Noel that reminded me of primary school.

He claimed to prefer the company of dogs to the company of women unless the woman in question was hideously ugly. Given his seeming addiction to the works of *John Waters*, I thought he was probably joking.

Noel would go to impossible lengths to wind people up. We were playing in a hall in a field thirty miles outside of Lismore. There were no visible lights or apparent signs of adjacent properties. God knows where the audience came from but I was getting big time "Deliverance" vibes.

When it came time for us to go on stage, I was told to go outside to find Noel. It was quiet out back; only the lowly moo of cattle. The calf looked up at me indignantly. Noel was readjusting his fly. I suspect it was a prank. I desperately hope it was a prank.

Stan Armstrong (who replaced Paul Gearside as *Psycho Surgeon* vocalist) recently saw a photo I posted of Noel on social media and, unprompted, told me he had once had to talk Noel out of fucking a cow. I'm beginning to think his powers of persuasion may not have been as successful as he imagined. Men are gross.

The gig ended about twelve minutes later when someone set fire to the stage. It was, however, quickly extinguished by the audience using their combined urine. Everyone's a critic.

THIRTY-FIVE
Hackney, London, 1981

Our next gig was in a pub somewhere in that once dread wasteland between Dalston Junction and Shoreditch. I walked down there in a group but I doubt I could even find the place again. I don't know how we got the gig. I can't remember the name of the pub and I never saw another band play there. We probably ruined any chance of that experiment happening again.

I could make a case that it never really happened; that it was a dream. I could erase it from this tale and no-one would ever need to know. I do, however, know it happened. I remember because we were unbelievably bloody awful.

And, as a reader, you should know that everything does not just go the way you think it should. Don't you just get fed up with people who tell these stories where every shit they touch turns to gold? I know so many people with such an overinflated sense of self-esteem that they can walk off a stage after delivering a performance that should be viewed in terms of complete humiliation and yet they glow with pride.

It's hard to really know what makes a performance fail so totally and utterly. Sometimes you get up there to play and just how the amps are placed makes the stage sound seem lack lustre even when the audience is hearing something completely different. This is especially true when amps are mic'd up but that wasn't the case here.

That night, the sound on stage wasn't great but I could still hear everything and everyone seemed to be going in different directions. It sounded like we were playing different songs and, worse still, we were playing them indifferently. Anything learnt in rehearsal seemed to vanish as cues were missed and there was a general feeling that no-one knew what the hell was going on. There was nothing to lock on to. I seemed to be the only person who was sober.

I pulled up the first song and said we're going to start again. Although it looks terrible on stage, that kind of extreme measure usually pulls everyone up and gets everyone on the same page because no-one wants to look like a dick.

If anything, the second attempt was worse than the first. There was no energy and no point. Seriously, if you can engage the audience, you can get away with anything on stage. Even if the audience despises you, you can still own something of the moment. This was as painful as watching a primary school violin ensemble massacre "*Silent Night.*"

There is nothing worse than standing on a stage with people who want it to end so they can collectively pretend it never happened. There is nothing worse than being boring and receiving polite applause. Our friends in the audience looked away so they wouldn't meet our gaze.

I felt the not so unusual feeling of shame. I wasn't used to feeling it on stage. After all the work and all the rehearsals, this ship was heading down to the bottom. Even the iceberg didn't want any part of it.

In the end, all I could do was smash my guitar in stupid blind fury. It didn't occur to me that there might at least be some kind of statement in doing so. I had not even considered that at least this was something to give the audience that they didn't see every day. No. It was just *"Hulk smash!"*

The guitar was an Aria Diamond (an incredibly light weight Japanese Mosrite rip off) and I loved it very much. It shattered spectacularly but even this could not save the show. I felt bereft and suicidal. I felt like an absolute fucking knob.

THIRTY-SIX
Bondi, Sydney, 1978

We had hired the old Masonic Hall on Bondi Road. It was a massive room with ornate wooden fixtures like an old-time school hall. It looked kind of haunted. Thick dust coated every surface and it felt like someone had died in there thirty years before and no-one had wanted to be caught dead there ever since.

We were waiting for *X* and they were making *Godot* look pretty damn prompt. *X* were not the Los Angeles band of the same name. We suspected they were probably sick and dirty; more dead than alive. As time ticked on, we were forced to consider if they had been forced to take a detour out to Lexington 125.

The natives, meanwhile, were getting pretty damn restless. They wanted those punk rock rhythms post haste.

Please, God. Don't let *X* hock the amps.

Doors had opened at 7:30pm and, for some unknown reason, the people had all come early. There had been a hundred people waiting for the door when it opened and then they just kept coming. Normally, you'd think that would be a pretty good sign if you'd hired a hall to make your Sydney debut. Not tonight, Josephine.

Unfortunately, we had chosen *X* to top the bill and they'd said they'd bring the PA. In fact, that was the main reason we'd invited *X* to play. They were getting kind of popular and they had a PA. None of this is rocket science.

We got there at the arranged time of 6pm and there was no sign of *X*. 8:30 came and went and there was still no sign of them. People began demanding we play. We had nothing to play through. We were a bunch of dicks holding guitars and looking fucking stupid.

There was fuck all that we could do about it either. Like everyone else, *X* didn't have a phone at their place. The mobile phone only existed if you worked for Dick Tracy.

They lived in Balmain when it was an underclass slum on the edge of the world. This was in the days when there was no Anzac Bridge and you crossed over to the other side via the two-lane Glebe Island Bridge. It was a swing bridge that would often bring Sydney traffic to a standstill to let the garbage scows pass through.

Back then, you could rent a three-story house in Darlinghurst for sixty bucks. You could rent a house in Glebe for forty-five. If you shopped around in Balmain, you could go maybe thirty.

The atmosphere turned thick and heavy with violence. Lynchings would begin promptly at 9:00. Ian Rilen finally arrived in foul mood two minutes before that dead line. He snarled and abused everyone in sight so that no-one would blame him for being late. A good offense is always the best defence unless you actually want to live in the world with other people.

We set up fast but there was no way we could set up fast enough for the crowd's liking. We were supposed to have run the songs past the stand in drummer at the sound check but that certainly wasn't going to happen. The whole thing was turning to shit. Before we played a note, we were hit by a torrent of abuse and empty beer cans by the audience.

Pete Tillman wasn't taking any shit from anyone. He reacted by hurling his microphone stand like a spear towards the back of the room. I watched it arc through the air in slow motion, thinking how this was going to end very badly. There was screaming. Obviously, that stand had hit someone.

Oh my God. He's already murdered someone.

Everything from that moment was going to be bad. Already someone was climbing up on stage. He headed straight towards Pete. Mad eyed, he had the face of someone contaminated by the kind of rage virus you see in those films where they don't want to use the word zombie. Pete dived straight at him and the impact caused both to vanish down the four-foot stage drop and into the crowd. I caught the odd flash of punches being thrown here and there.

Everything was beginning to look like television coverage of the Vietnam war.

The audience's retribution began in earnest as barely the first notes had been played. They initially stepped up their game by switching from empties to full cans and bottles.

Heavier objects quickly followed, starting with chairs and broken bits of railing. It quickly intensified to entire rows of chairs.

Three van loads of broken furnishings were dumped on Bondi Beach that night as we tried to hide the worst of the damage from the Masons.

Bondi Masonic Hall obviously means it was owned and operated by the Masons. The guys with the handshakes and the three distinct knocks.

I'm not stupid. I know that when you defile the temple of a secret society, there will be consequences. They'll do their secret gestures and invisible doors will quietly close. The glass ceiling will be lowered several notches.

I'd like to say that it was their iron hand in the velvet glove that has kept me from scaling the peaks to which I aspired. It would, however, be a lie. My life has been a mess of my own making and, still, I regret nothing.

Or, at least, I pretend to regret nothing.

THIRTY-SEVEN
Stoke Newington, London, 1981

In the aftermath of the gig, Ruthless was gone. There was no way she'd hang around after that level of defeat and incompetence. We'd have to find a new bass player and who the fuck would want to play with us after that abominable display.

I needed a new guitar but I wasn't exactly flushed for funds. I lucked out and found a no-name hollow body guitar in a Stoke Newington pawn shop. It looked like a rip on a Gibson S355 but it had been stripped of its electrics.

The shop was selling it for 12 quid but I got them to knock it down to eight. At least the neck was thin and straight.

I managed to install the P90s out of the ruins of my old guitar. The wiring, the pickups and the knobs had held together in one piece so it was just a matter of fixing it to the holes. It worked but the damn thing screamed like a banshee strangling a cat. I stuffed its guts with toilet paper and that tamed the feedback down to a manageable level.

This Frankenstein of a guitar would go on to play all the early *Blood and Roses* gigs and it appears on all the *Kamera Records* recordings. It literally was a piece of junk. But punk rock doesn't necessarily come from fancy pants equipment.

It was a Sunday afternoon and we went to Brockwell Park just south of Brixton to see *Stiff Little Fingers* play a *Rock against Racism* gig. The skinhead terror has been unrelenting for months, unreported by media and ignored by authority. We came to see the band but we knew the skins were coming for us. The intelligence had been coming in all afternoon; sightings, gossip and reported threats.

In the months and years leading up to that day, we had all been beaten, robbed or worse. You can always run and you can always hide but it is not a great way to live your life. People will give you a thousand reasons not to let you live your life the way you want to. We could go safely home or we could take a chance. I dropped some speckled blues and I waited. A lot of other people did the same.

I could feel the electric rush travel up my spine as the speed came on. The band was on the side of the stage waiting to play. We were crushed against the front barriers; a quivering of anticipation.

To the north, I saw the push and shove of the bald phalanx moving forward towards us. They shouted *"Zeig Heil"* and made the requisite inappropriate salutes. They did not, however, get very far. This was a park in Brixton after all and Nazis weren't exactly popular with the locals. This had been a very poor strategy on their part. A lot of people think Rastas are all dope and peace but Yardies were straight up gangster.

Within ten seconds, the skinheads were retreating as fast as their bovver booted legs could carry them. It was a long way back to the tube station but they made it in record time. Tails between legs, clouds of dust in their wake, run out on a rail; gone.

The guitar introduction of *Alternative Ulster* cut through the sudden still of the afternoon air. The speed and the drums cut in and we danced as though we were at the best party the world had ever thrown. It had been a long time coming but a change had finally come.

And, here in that moment, it was clear why music was so important. Here was the feeling punk rock was supposed to share. A freedom from fear.

THIRTY-EIGHT
Sydney, 1978

When *Filth* played there were fights every time. No sooner had the guitars been plugged in, someone would emerge from the crowd to attempt to rid us from the world. It was unbelievable that we could create such a reaction by simply turning up. The hatred was real and it gave us power.

In between brawls, Pete sang like Frank Sinatra over the racket. It was an eerie sound and, as I predicted, the audience just loathed him. The band reacted by playing worse. You didn't like that? Okay. Here's something you'll really hate. In all fairness, the audience had every right to want to destroy us. They seemed to spend time and money just for the opportunity to do so. Perhaps, for better effect, they just could have let us get started before launching their attack.

This had become more akin to performance art than anything about music. Performance art would not have been a concept we would be acquainted with. This was just a dumb idea and we were kind of running with it because it was fun. There. I said it.

Pete wanted to wear a straitjacket on stage. He didn't want a pretend one. He wanted a certified psych ward special. Of course, we didn't know such things had become obsolete in the world of modern psychotherapy because we learnt how medicine worked at the movies. Why bother strapping someone up when you could stick a syringe full of Largactil in their butt cheek or roll them up in a mattress?

Pete got me to take him to Sydney Hospital where we made the case that he was infected by a plot twist like the *Incredible Hulk* or the *Werewolf of London*. We needed a straitjacket to restrain him from the dramatic transformation caused by the full moon. He needed to be restrained for the safety of society.

Pete gave a performance right on a par with *Lon Chaney Jr* in the Wolfman. Yes. It was that unconvincing.

Of course, we left empty handed. In hindsight, I realise the psychiatrist probably thought this was some kind of sex thing. After all, we were only a couple of blocks North of Oxford Street.

The weird thing was that we'd suddenly play a professional (and I use that term loosely) sounding gig completely out of the blue (but generally completely without Noel). We played one gig at the Governor Bourke Hotel in Camperdown where we did seventeen songs in about half an hour. They were clearly songs. They had all their noticeable bits in the appropriate places. It wasn't that different to the *Ramones*.

We finished our first set and the audience was stunned. Then they pulled their chins up off of the floor, cheered, roared and wanted to bear our children.

Unfortunately, we were still expected to play for another hour and we had run out of songs. The next set had to consist of one very long version of *Louie Louie*. It started off okay and went quickly downhill from there. We only managed about forty minutes but, by then, the pub was completely empty. The publican barred us for our collective lives and then at least we felt vindicated.

The straight press jumped on board with articles and outrage. Being infamous was better than being rich. Every day brought new chaos into our lives. We had a gig with the *Psycho Surgeons* at a North Sydney High School. I was sick with a raging fever. I knocked back a shit ton of ephedrine and just figured I'd be all right. The show, after all, must go on.

This guy called *Barrie Earl* had come up from Melbourne with various members of the *Boys Next Door* (soon to be the *Birthday Party*). He said he wanted to sign us up for his brand spanking new label called *Suicide Records.* He hadn't even heard us.

Suicide Records was an attempt by the Australian music industry to cash in on the latest craze. The feather in his cap was the *Boys Next Door* but he'd essentially scooped up every band in their orbit. One of those bands was the *Teenage Radio Stars* who recorded what they claimed was an original song called "*I Wanna Be Your Baby*". It was in fact a semi reworded cover of the *Vibrators*' "*Baby, Baby*". That will tell you enough about their punk rock credibility.

Pete took one look at the fat old fuck and threw a chair at him. As mister music biz ran for his life, we climbed up on stage and began to play something that resembled our version of the *Stooges*' *LA Blues*. We wanted him to know just how shit we could be if we really put our minds to it. He went back home with a contract with *Wasted Days*. I would have said wasted trip but the resulting record sales made such a statement superfluous.

About ten seconds into that gig, I realised that the ephedrine was not actually going to cut it. I face planted onto the floor, busting all the machine heads on one side of the guitar. I was left flaying around the floor hitting the guitar with the metal chain I used as a strap. I kept running through a mantra of *"The show must go on, the show must go on."*

Pete dived into the crowd. He writhed and rolled and bit people's ankles.

National current affairs magazine *"The Bulletin"* wrote a review that described our set as little more than an extension of tuning up. We were superstars.

THIRTY-NINE
Stoke Newington, 1981

For those without an ideological connection to a notion of what punk could be, a quick change of clothing ultimately meant very little. If the price of not getting the crap beaten out of you was a shaved head and a Fred Perry shirt, there were going to be a couple of barbers and merchants near Petticoat Lane who had finally come out of economic recession.

Besides, if you had no real discernment about the noise you were listening to, the football chants of the *"Oi!"* brigade could always fill that hole in your heart for crude, thrashy music.

The influence of politics on a lot of the early punks had been largely overstated. Obviously, there were exceptions that proved this rule but punk had exploded with little more than a dress code and a shared discontent. There were kids who had signed onto the punk bandwagon because they had just bought a copy of the *Stranglers'* great revolutionary opus: *"Peaches"*. A genre that was broad enough to accommodate that was not going to be a vehicle for social change.

By mid-Seventy-Seven, it almost seemed like everybody and their pet dog had become a punk (at least they had done so on the odd weekend or at a kinky suburban party).

This had not led to any real rise in political consciousness (at least not in a radical left-wing sense). *The Jam*'s *Paul Weller* had told us he would vote Tory. He did and continued to do so until it suited him to do otherwise. His sudden turn to the socialist fold seemed to mimic the fortunes of his record sales and the criticisms of the *NME*.

Up until this point, there had been very few punks who had seriously believed in a system of social organisation based on equality and the removal of all power structures. Anarchy had merely meant getting pissed and destroying whatever shit wasn't nailed down. As the seventies became the eighties, that was changing too. There were things called books and some of us actually read them.

We were based around Stoke Newington now, perilously avoiding eviction from housing co-operatives. Even with peppercorn rents, life on the dole made living tight. For a start, there was no local supermarket and we found ourselves at the mercy of price gouging local stores. It should be no surprise that, if you are poor, you pay more for everything.

When you have sod all money, you buy smaller amounts. Smaller amounts always cost more per item than purchasing in bulk. If you are poor you end up using a less efficient heating technology. Being poor keeps you poor.

When Governments talk about the cost of living, they take into account things like mortgage payments and interest rates. Prices might double in your local store but they're going to tell you everyone is better off because interest rates are down half a percent. The price of a television has come down. There'll be no increase to Social Security rates because the things you can't afford cost less than they did before.

At first, we were in Batley Road, conveniently opposite the local police station. This pretty much guaranteed plenty of engagement with local law enforcement. Seriously, if you are poor and you had not been kicked in the head by a horse as a child, you understood the reality of day-to-day oppression.

You'd walk down the street and the cops would empty your pockets. Hell, I've been strip searched in the street and just felt lucky they didn't charge me with public indecency.

One night we all had acid and I was fairly certain it had no effect on me other than finding the peculiarities of human gestures more amusing than normal. It was certainly less mind blowing that I had been told to expect. Then, I flicked a light switch and there was a power failure in the entire immediate area. To this day, I wonder if the power outage was real or a figment of my imagination. If it was a figment, I believe I may have underestimated my own imagination.

Death seemed to continue to follow us. One morning, we heard screaming from a neighbouring house as well as flames and smoke pouring out of the window. We broke down the front door only to find a burnt woman in the corridor. She was clearly dead with smoke leaving her lungs accompanied by the unmistakable death rattle.

A month or so later, we moved into a different house around the corner in Yoakley Road. This place was special in that there was no way to get the water on. The mains supply had been cut before any tap and a lead pipe bent protruding from the wall had been bent over upon itself to stop the flow from the outside world.

We managed to get the plumbing in. Plumbing isn't rocket science no matter what a plumber charges you. It's pretty much pre soldered Lego that you just run a torch over. The trouble was, no-one (including the Housing Co-operative) wanted to help with finding a way to connect copper pipe to lead. This was, obviously, a recipe for hell on Earth.

Clissold Park was about a kilometre up the road so, every morning, I'd get up and walk there with an empty twenty-litre bottle. I'd do what was necessary in the public toilets and then fill the bottle from a garden tap. I would then take the now full bottle back to Yoakley Road. I'd then repeat this journey a couple of more times with other bottles in the hope that there would be water for cooking and flushing the toilet.

Unfortunately, not everybody could get on board with this practice. Not naming any names but there were some subhuman fucking animals who, by all evidence, couldn't even shit straight whilst squatting over an eighteen-inch pile of human faeces.

To make matters worse, Richard (did I mention a name?) had a dog. Richard didn't walk the dog or clean up after the dog. He clearly did feed the dog because the evidence was clearly fucking everywhere. This dumb fuck of a dog even shat on the stairs.

Medieval writers had a propensity to describe hell and all its horrors. They had no idea. They at least tossed their excrement into the street. I was stuck in a shit encrusted hell that not even God or the Devil could have imagined. I considered gaol as a preferred option. Maybe even a religious order.

One morning, there was a banging on the door and repeated pathetic cries to be let in. It was Richard and it was very early. He was very much the worse for wear having obviously over indulged his senses with whatever chemical was in fashion. Naked as the day I was born, I stumbled out of bed. I needed to shut Richard up so that I could return to my ancient slumbers. I winced at the first light of the summer dawn like some Nosferatu motherfucker.

As I approached the door, I felt one of the dog's little calling cards slip between my toes. The soft warm horror of it. The sudden awareness that I would not be able to return to bed. Shit had murdered sleep.

I was not pleased. I found myself seized by a furious anger and I set forth to smite down my enemy with great vengeance. Gathering Richard from the stoop, I proceeded to rub his nose in any shit I could find. There was a lot of shit for me to find. Thinking back, that must have been a terrifying sight.

I told you, I'm not the good guy in this story.

After about six weeks of unspeakable and unsanitary horror, funds were secured to have the water turned off in the road and a stopcock welded to the mains supply. After some particularly gruesome cleaning the house became habitable. I may have bathed for a month, scrubbing at the long-forgotten nooks and crannies of my body. All evidence of this trauma needed to be removed.

It was to be a short-lived respite from horror. On Christmas Eve, a large group of skinheads arrived without warning, kicking open the front door. I was able to move fairly quickly, pushing over a wardrobe so it blocked the door. With the added weight of everybody else in the room, we were secure.

We were on the ground floor, so I positioned myself next to the back window with a heavy blunt object in my hand. Having never quite gotten over the invasions of Campbell Buildings, I still usually left heavy blunt objects in accessible positions.

Upstairs, the terrible sounds of violence reigned down; smashing glass and screams. The people who lived upstairs were doing far worse up there than we were. We had essentially retreated into the medieval concept of a keep. Feeling guilt, I wanted to go upstairs but that was absurd. Whilst we remained in the eye of the storm, the tempest was far from over.

FORTY
Bondi Junction, Sydney, 1978

The way my brain is wired makes a lot of things complicated. It's true that I can watch a mystery film and guess the ending in the first ten minutes. I can do this so well that I prefer to watch an unintelligible Giallo to its predictable British or American cousin. Their non-sensical endings at least mean I'm kept guessing.

I can walk into a room and immediately identify the complicated web of human relationships. Just don't ask me to walk into a party and understand what the hell I'm supposed to be doing there. In my younger days, I would become a performing monkey but, these days, I'll just stand in a corner until someone tells me it's time to go home.

I find watching American movies where young people party with their hands in the air rather confusing as I don't think I've ever seen this as an existing phenomenon. If I were to walk into a place where that was happening, I'd flee in abject horror.

I also find it extraordinarily hard to relate to multiple friends. People have peculiar competing interactions. They want you to keep secrets including those that work against the interest of other friends. I can understand these Machiavellian ploys when I can observe them as an outsider. When I am forced to engage in these machinations, my brain tends to short circuit, often blathering unwanted truths and causing awkward social interactions.

It was a Saturday afternoon and *X* were playing a free gig at the Mill Hill Hotel in Bondi Junction. These days, like much of Inner-City Sydney, this part of town is considered fairly up market. Back in the late seventies, it was still fairly working class and unforgiving of the strange and unusual.

Looking around the room, one could clearly see the natives were more than restless; they were planning murder. I mentioned this to my companions and they said, quite frankly, they couldn't see it. I completely failed to see how they couldn't see it. Hadn't they ever seen a cat stalk a bird?

These were the days when people went to work and chucked their dogs out into the street and the dogs would form packs and wander the neighbourhood. Hadn't these guys ever walked to school and had to negotiate these packs?

It was sure as shit they'd never gone to a High School in Figtree.

So, I said to my friends "When the band stops playing, we need to get the fuck out of here before it turns into a bloodbath."

"Sure," they said but they weren't listening. The band stopped playing and I walked out onto Oxford Street but no-one joined me. I waited a minute. I waited two minutes. I waited five minutes. I waited just knowing the roof was about to get torn off the place.

There I was, feeling guilty but safe on the pavement. A voice kept telling me I should go in there and persuade my friends to leave as soon as humanly possible. The voice grew louder; a nagging near suicidal voice that demanded loyalty.

Like an idiot, I walked back in only to cop the first sucker punch thrown. I was hit so hard, I hit the floor before I knew I'd even been punched. I looked up, trying to work out what all these weird lines were before realising they were chair legs and I was looking up towards the ceiling. My face was vibrating. Someone was on top of me wailing down blow after blow. I could offer no resistance. I waited for death.

FORTY-ONE
Stoke Newington, London 1981

So, we needed a bass player and Richard knew this guy. I don't know what his real name was but we called him Clapham. He lived in Clapham and he wanted to be called Clapham. So, we called him Clapham.

Now, the guy could play. The trouble was, he didn't know when to stop playing. It was like he was constantly playing a solo full of two octave runs. You had Richard doing these Burundi variation beats and these long wanks of bass playing that didn't slot into any kind of groove. It was all fill and no thrill but I kind of learnt to work with it because we had a bass player and this was a step back towards being an actual band.

Some of this sound can be heard on the "*Life After Death*" cassette. We recorded the band on a cassette recorder through the in-built condenser microphone. We then crudely multi-tracked vocals over the top by playing the cassette through a home stereo whilst Lisa sang in front of another cassette recorder. At least we were beginning to grasp how the concept of recording worked in the most unlikely DIY way possible.

There was a free outdoor festival in Clissold Park and they asked for local acts to play. Much to our surprise, someone on the local council heard the rather primitive demo tape and still said yes. The only thing we had to do was give them a name because they weren't going to have a band play that didn't have a name no matter what artistic explanation we provided.

A *Cramps* song was on the radio. *Lux Interior* delivered the line "*ABCDEFG, you're gonna hear from me.*" *ABCDEFG* became our name or, at least, the place holder for a name.

We were forced outside of our natural environment. There was that most hated thing; sunshine. On stage, we felt its cruel burn. We were not made to play in daylight. There were no shadows to hide in. This was not an atmosphere we found conducive to the kind of show we wanted to deliver.

Mercifully, however, we sounded okay. We sounded better than okay. The audience didn't seem to hate us. They applauded and made appreciative noises in all the right places. It may have been the turning point we were waiting for.

I knew we needed to get rid of Clapham but I wasn't going to say anything. In bands, I always thought that, even if you weren't entirely convinced of the hand you were dealt, you kind of worked to build around the structure and maybe find something unexpected.

More ruthless hands prevailed. Clapham was out and Jez was in. Lisa was far more practical than I was. The turnaround was so swift and decisive that I suspect other elements might have been in play that I was unaware of.

I would perhaps speculate that a drug deal may have gone astray.

FORTY-TWO
Alexandria, Sydney, 1978

Most of *Filth*'s gigs were taking place upstairs in a warehouse in Alexandria largely used as the *Psycho Surgeons*' rehearsal room. I think there was a printer downstairs and the building may have had something to do with Mark Taylor's parent's business. I didn't ask questions. There was a room and we could play there.

A small but vocal crowd became regulars. Most Saturday nights a fairly interesting parade of freaks and weirdos made the fifteen-minute walk down from Redfern Station to these parties/happenings.

The most notorious of these events was one that I have come to call the "*Baptism of Blood*".

The Psycho Surgeons were about to release a single called "*Horizontal Action*" with "*Wild Weekend*" on The B-side. They were piled up in boxes in plain white paper sleeves. There was another pile of plain white cardboard outer sleeves and there were two large plastic bottles filled with blood.

Mark insisted the blood was human and illegally purchased from a technician working in Sydney University. This was not true. Forensic tests by Sydney Police later established it was cow blood. Mark, however, had said it was human blood and Pete Tillman and I were prepared to go along with that.

Clotheslines had been strung across wooden supports and the cardboard outer sleeves were being decorated individually in blood with various decorative splashes, splatters and hand prints. These were then pegged on the lines to dry. The room smelled like an abattoir.

When the artwork was complete, there was still a fair amount of blood left. Certainly, there was enough to fuel a huge number of nightmares for many years to come.

Before the gig, I wrote up a manifesto for *Filth*. It was reprinted on the handbill. Knowing my history lessons, I nailed a copy of the Manifesto on the front door of the Offices of *RAM* in homage to *Martin Luther* and the All Saints' Church in Wittenberg. There was a sense we were working towards something big but it was still not a fully formed idea.

The set had been a straight forward event up until that point. We'd made an unbearable racket. Pete had thrown himself down the stairs a couple of times. It was all pretty much business as usual.

Except there was this bottle of blood on the side of the stage. We had kind of been dared to use it to some theatrical effect but I think no-one was quite prepared for just how far things would go. Ten litres of blood. A pack of idiots on stage being dared to do something stupid. What could possibly go wrong?

We started playing a cover of the *Velvet Underground*'s "*White Light/White Heat*". If you listened closely, you may have recognised it. After thrashing around randomly across the entire length of the guitar's neck, I had managed to destroy a number of strings and the bass and drums thundered on to the low wail of feedback.

I grasped hold of the bottle and reached over to the microphone.

"*This is human blood*," I said and cracked open the lid of the bottle. A certain amount of unease rose up from the crowd and quite justifiably so. I could just randomly splash it out onto the audience. That was definitely something *Filth* might do. Everyone must have seen *Carrie* by then so I think most people could imagine the possibilities the future might hold.

People drew back, many retreating towards the back wall. Already there were screams of horror. I was essentially bluffing thinking maybe I'd pour a splash on the space on the floor that had opened up before the stage. I thought the room would clear, big joke, no damage done.

Having attended a Baptist church I thought I'd throw in a bit of that old time preacher talk about being washed in the blood of the lamb. That should have been enough to frighten off anyone.

My bluff was quickly called as one guy walked to the front of the stage and knelt down with his arms in a Jesus Christ pose. What could I do? There was no way to back down. I was committed to the character.

I thought I'd just pour a bit on his head and he'd have had

enough. Let me tell you, if you've ever had a nose bleed, you'll know a little bit of blood goes a very long way.

The difficulty of manipulating a large plastic bottle of blood was immediately apparent as considerably more than a nosebleed worth of liquid hit his forehead. I'm thinking at least a cup's worth.

It went a very, very long way.

Worse yet, other people had entered the fray. They came to join the anointed one in near religious fervour. Suddenly, it was a born again bona fide according to *Hoyle* miracle. People were writhing on the bloody floor as if possessed by demons. There was a wailing and gnashing of teeth. They spoke in tongues. It was a *Ken Russell* horror movie come to life.

To this day, I am surprised I did not unleash a plague that could have taken out ninety-nine-point nine percent of life on Planet Earth. We got lucky this time, people. Let's not try that again.

FORTY-THREE
Stoke Newington, London, 1981

Jez played with an essential *Ramones* palate and that immediately shifted the band into something more exciting. I had also been writing songs that were very much built on bass lines. I may not have been overly impressed by the *Stranglers'* lyrics but those bass riffs were pretty inspiring.

Rather than fiddle and blur the edge as Clapham had done, Jez locked into them and that locked in with the drums. Suddenly, we had a certain necessary bottom end thump. Jez also fitted in and it began to feel more like a gang.

He did, however, make a strong claim to having working class roots even though his father was a university lecture and he was somehow related to Singaporean Prime Minister Lee Kuan Yew.

His drug problems were also far worse than any of us realised.

Lisa also had her habits but these seemed largely under control and within recreational tolerance. She was the daughter of a minister and, prior to her arrival at Campbell Buildings, had served out a six-month sentence at Holloway.

Richard had emerged from some south London shithole and had no desire to return to the suburban hell that spawned him. He also had more than a passing interest in drugs and alcohol.

I won't lie and tell you I had no problem with substance abuse. Generally, however, I could be diverted. If I kept myself engaged in artistic matters, I generally felt no need to obliterate myself. I did, however, discover that opiates could focus my head in ways other drugs didn't.

Codeine, in particular, allowed me to pull all-nighters without any lack of quality control. Codeine was fairly easy to obtain as chemist's still sold it in linctus form without prescription. Pure codeine tablets called DF 118s were fairly easily available on the black market as they were not really regarded as a sin at the time. Hell, at the time, you could still buy kaolin and morphine solution over the counter and it didn't take a genius to separate out the chalk powder.

Eventually, future governments and medical organisations would decide these things were indeed sinful and moved to ban them accordingly. Apparently, sin is not absolute and writ large in stone by God. It seemed Church and State had some say in the matter.

I did find myself pulling all-nighters as correspondence began to increase. As the band played more, the written requests for fanzine interviews grew. I became the de-facto voice of the band largely because no-one else could be bothered. And I was a big mouth and that didn't hurt. I was getting daily requests for live tapes and articles. I spent hours individually copying tapes onto tapes in real time.

Not that I minded. Hyperfocus is my best friend. It's a pure dopamine hit all of its own. It also allowed me to shape the band in my own image. I'd make suggestions and, in the beginning, the others would just rubber stamp them. Essentially, a lunatic had his hand on the tiller.

It had become easier to accept that the band needed a name as having no name had gotten us very little traction. Clearly art house conceits would not fly in an environment that was far straighter and more ruled by commerce than it gave itself credit.

The important thing was to have a name that didn't have the baggage of everyone else's music. There was agreement that it should reflect both masculine and feminine; violence and beauty. These were the vague terms we tossed around as we tried to line up appropriate words into a concept.

Roger Vadim's "*Blood and Roses*" was a film that had really struck me as a youngster. *Vadim* is perhaps best known for "*And God Created Woman*" and "*Barberella*". His work has a unique visual style that often takes precedent over storytelling.

"*Blood and Roses*" was notorious for its lesbian themes though the presentation of these were pretty much tame even at the time of release. I suspect a modern viewer might not pick up on them at all. Certainly, Hammer's Carmilla trilogy (based on the same short story by *Sheridan Le Fanu*) is noticeably more lurid.

Carl Theodor Dreyer's *Vampyr* used the source material to more surrealistic but less erotic effect in 1931.

Blood and Roses had been screened in its entirety on one of *Bill Collins'* late night movie screenings on *Channel Nine* and it was shown at a very late time in the evening. It was three o'clock in the morning on a school night. So, it was also on very early.

What had most impressed me about the film was a dream sequence where the action changed to black and white with splashes of red. This is certainly the best scene in the movie but was often entirely excised from international cuts of the film.

This sudden piece of surrealism had really opened my mind in terms of storytelling and the interaction between dreams and reality. Much of what I have created has been dragged wholesale from dreams.

This concept of a blurring between reality and dreams had recently become something I really was becoming obsessed by. There was a field near Figtree High School and, whenever I had a severe asthma attack, I would dream there was an abandoned church in the middle of it, filled with terrible monsters.

Asthma dreams are quite often extremely repetitive and memorable in their suffocating feel. It probably explained my obsession with the music of the *Velvet Underground* and the *Stooges*. Asthma attacks also reminded me of the short blistering guitar riff on *John Lennon*'s *Cold Turkey*. If you ever see the sheet music for that song, there's a notation to repeat those bars 49 times. That is what asthma feels like.

By the time I was back in London, I had pretty much forgotten about this recurring figment of the boarded-up ghost church. It was gone from my head, not even a memory of a memory. There was also Ventolin now. It had allowed me to say goodbye to certain childhood things and nightmares.

However, in Stoke Newington, just around the corner from Yoakley Road, there was Abney Park Cemetery. In the centre of the graveyard there was a long-abandoned church. Actually, it wasn't an abandoned church, it was the abandoned church or at least something close enough to the dream to re-install ancient memory.

The reptile brain seeks refuge in the supernatural. Dreams made impossibly real were not comforting.

Lyrically, I had already begun using occult themes as a kind of way to sidle on up to a political idea. My first attempt had been a song called *"Night of the Living Dead"* which was so banal it immediately found its way into a rubbish bin. But actual songs eventually did get written.

"Spit on your Grave" was about censorship and oppression by the religious right. *"Love Under Will"* was about stepping away from addictions through artistic expression. *"Jesus"* and *"Your Sin is your Salvation"* were straight up rejections of Christian faith.

These were ideas that had already taken root within our social milieu. Later, wider audiences often seemed to misunderstand this, adding an unfortunate kind of fantasy interpretation.

Dreams, however, will not be contained within a single, simple meaning. You unleash them at your peril.

Somehow, out of these musings, the name *Blood and Roses* came to be.

FORTY-FOUR
Alexandria, Sydney, 1978

There was a coup and Noel was gone. Elvis and Pete had petitioned for a real drummer. I wasn't sure that was the point we were trying to make and Noel was probably the guy I most talked to in the band.

The thing was, I came to a rehearsal and Martin was there and Noel wasn't. I didn't know in advance and no-one had told Noel because they were expecting me to put the knife in next time I saw him. *"He's out. You tell him."* Bands can be a fucking toxic place to hang your hat.

There were gigs coming up in Adelaide; an actual tour. I was urged to at least try what it would sound like. I suspect the three of them had already rehearsed together because Martin seemed to know all the stops and starts in a way you could never have anticipated if you'd heard Noel drumming.

It worked. It was easy. We had been working so fucking hard at sounding so fucking awful. Being a regular punk rock band was embarrassingly simple but we didn't just sound like a regular punk band. We sounded like a fucking great punk band. Those wild screeching noise breaks rained down like hurricanes. The fait was totally accompli.

There were, however, other problems. One of the main ones was something that followed me around through a number of bands.

I increasingly found that I didn't want to hang around with the boys. I preferred hanging out with girls.

Here's the problem. Modern society is clear that men and women should be treated the same. The trouble with this argument is that men talk about boring shit and want to do stupid things. If you don't believe me, throw a ball out into the middle of the road when there are a group of men around and see what happens. They're like puppies with a stick.

In addition, if I'm in a relationship with a woman, I find my attention is immediately focused on her. You cannot distract me by kicking over dustbins, throwing paint at walls, climbing fences or pissing against trees. I have more interesting things to do with my time. None of them involve sport or acting like a dick.

Many guys in bands like to direct the word Yoko at your significant other when you refuse to pay attention to their boorish behaviour. A certain amount of tension arose when the band wouldn't let me bring my girlfriend on tour. They said that they would have to take their girlfriends if I took mine. For a variety of reasons, many involving personal hygiene, the rhythm section didn't actually have girlfriends.

It was late May of 78 when we drove off towards Adelaide. There had been a last-minute minor complication that arose that endangered our many rehearsals. The afternoon we were set to leave, Elvis had been locked up in his bedroom by his parents and was not allowed out. They had literally put a lock on his door to keep him in. It can never be easy.

FORTY-FIVE
Kings Cross, London, 1982

I think, perhaps, in the Sixties and early Seventies, when the music business was run by old men with old school ties, the record companies were a little more open to who they'd sign and promote. Those cigar chomping suits didn't have a clue about what the kids were in to. Some very left field figures managed to not only be signed but also to get airplay through record company muscle.

Punk had brought about the independent record boom but that merely meant the big companies didn't have to take so many chances. They could move in and acquire anything that broke through.

Additionally, independent music found itself shifted to the ghettos of late-night radio. It found itself at the mercy of a whole new breed of gatekeepers; people convinced they knew exactly what the kids not so much wanted but needed. A ruthless cadre of style police fighting for their own agendas.

So, we were playing this pub called New Merlin's Cave in Kings Cross and we were pretty pleased with ourselves. As a band, this was as close to the West End as we'd ever managed to come. We were playing and there were people who wanted to see us including people we didn't actually know. This was about as far up the ladder as we had ever imagined going.

We'd kind of rode in on the tailcoats of fanzine writers who had scored work in the straight music press. There'd been reviews here and there. There'd even been letters from Indie record labels but none of them had played out into actual interest. Simply put, once they heard us or saw us, all interest died. We were grotty and wore the vague air of the criminally insane. We were an open book best judged by its cover.

We'd just played a support gig to The Playn Jayn over in Kensington at the Ad Lib Club. Our friends had all turned up and made it abundantly clear they didn't think the headliners should go on after us and we should return to the stage. Our friends were as dishevelled and bad mannered as us and we were promptly banned from the pub based entirely on the riff raff we attracted. This had caused at least one record company to lose all interest.

I think their actual main concern was the sight of Alistair Livingstone of *Kill Your Pet Puppy* and the *Encyclopedia of Ecstasy* fame performing a go-go dance on stage in pink tights and tutu. I was asked if this was a regular occurrence. I patiently explained that we didn't really like to draw a line between performer and audience and thought the proscenium arch interfered with the ritualistic nature of our events.

That scared him off.

We were proud of our untouchable status. When you get rejected enough, it becomes a badge of honour. Your mere survival in the face of indifference becomes a cause for celebration. The world squashes people tougher than us every single day and yet, here we were, still standing.

At this stage, I kind of figured we'd never get a record out. We were far too hopeless to put out a record by ourselves even if we had pulled together some money. We were way beneath pulling money out of the music business. The music business just kept on finding new ways to take money off of us. Ever wonder why so many ex-musicians ran rehearsal rooms, recording studios and equipment hire?

There was a shit ton more money to be made out of that than being a jobbing musician.

Suddenly, there was this guy called Saul who wanted to talk to me. He says he was from *Kamera Records* but that meant sweet fuck all to me. He kept asking questions about where I envisioned the band heading. I thought he was taking the piss.

Instead of giving an accurate and more usual reply along the lines of "*nowhere fast*" or "*to hell in a handbasket*", I responded with utterly ludicrous suggestions along the lines of touring the world, British number ones and headlining Wembley Stadium. Any idiot could spot I had my sarcasm dial turned up to the heart of the sun. I side winked knowing looks across the table to people who were desperately trying to hold back laughter.

Bizarrely, these answers (which if taken seriously would have identified me as a delusional narcissist) seemed to be very the words he actually wanted to hear. It does sometimes occur to me that it is easier to get on in your life if you grease the wheels with bullshit. The problem then is getting the bullshit off of your hands.

Before we'd even played, he was talking about drawing up a contract.

More surprisingly, even after he had heard us, he didn't tear it up.

FORTY-SIX
Adelaide, South Australia, 1978

Unlike previous trips out of town, this time, we were in big V8 cars hired for the occasion. It's hard to explain the size of Australia to Europeans. Adelaide is about 1400kms away from Sydney. This is like going from London to Budapest without any major cities in between.

In a car, there is very little to do except get on each other's nerves. You didn't hire a V8 to show off or advertise any inadequacy in your underpants. You hired a V8 to improve your chances of crossing the very wasteland they would soon film Mad Max in.

The sudden absence of Elvio created certain unforeseen difficulties. *Filth* had rebuilt itself into a tight, efficient punk band that played a vicious effective 12 song set that could be performed in under twenty-five minutes. We were bad, mad and dangerous to know.

Mark Taylor of the *Psycho Surgeons* said he would step in and do double duty. We arrived at an import record shop in Hindley Street. We ran the set and everyone was positive. The small mob of vinyl enthusiasts that haunted the racks voiced their approval.

Then we went to the Governor Hindmarsh Hotel and things quickly turned to shit. This was to be the opening night for the venue and the sound on stage seemed incomprehensible. It was possibly because this was the first time we'd played through mic'ed amps and the only thing we were getting back through the foldback was vocals. This was entirely outside our experience.

I don't know what it sounded like out front but, on stage, it sounded unbelievably fucking awful. The one thing *Filth* did know how to do when things sounded awful was to act as badly as we possibly could. Abuse audience members for their indifference; check. Walk on tables; check. Get thrown out of the pub; check. Get barred from every pub date on the tour; check mate.

This time, however, we seemed to have crossed some kind of Rubicon of bad behaviour. It wasn't just the music press who had pricked up their ears; it was actual daily newspapers. You can always find a small enough pond to cause a stir if you look hard enough. They were sending reporters and photographers. The world had literally gone batshit insane. *ABC*, the National Broadcaster, was even sending a camera crew.

We had all the smart arse replies they could possibly ask for.

"The publican said he had people working behind the bar who could play better than you."

"He probably does but who wants to listen to that kind of old people crap?"

All the insults that they threw at us, we accepted happily as compliments. We relished in our bad behaviour. To top it off, we looked hotter than the Clash in the photos. Skinny, crop haired and insolent; we had somehow, in our blundering incompetence, captured the zeitgeist.

FORTY-SEVEN
London, 1982

The big London punk gigs seemed largely monopolised by what I would politely call the more blokey purveyors of punk. Since *"Adam and the Ants"* had gone pop and *"Killing Joke"* had become massive, the Sunday night shows at the Lyceum had largely become the domain of *"The Exploited"*, *"The Anti Nowhere League"* and their ilk. If you wore boots, they'd make you leave your laces at the door. That was the audience they had grown to expect.

This offshoot of punk was more a seeming return to a more rock-based aesthetic than their haircuts and costumes indicated. It was a genre slinking back into the sexism and homophobia of a time thought long passed. The intermixing with bald heads and bovver boots also suggested the underlining casual racism that even these bands had at least learnt to shy away from in public.

An alternative had begun to spring up, initially at the Autonomy Centre in Wapping and then the Centro Iberico on Harrow Road. These Sunday gigs began to attract larger audiences and, with the boneheads at the Lyceum, they attracted very little trouble.

It was a little weird going to Wapping for the first time. The Autonomy Centre was on Wapping Wall, a brief walk down Wapping High Street from the Underground Station.

At the time, the idea that the High Street had ever been a place of commerce seemed absurd. It was little more than a lane surrounded by hoardings. The hoardings hid ruins and holes in the ground. Thirty-five years after World War 2, the bombsites were still the only thing left of what once had been a community.

This was the street my Grandparents had settled in after fleeing Ireland.

"*Blood and Roses*" were fairly much welded to the Anarcho-punk scene through social interaction. Our music was not really representative of the scene as such. There would, for example, be no place for our music on the Crass label. We had our own thing but we shared the same hovels.

This was, however, the social setting we found ourselves most comfortable in and, as I often said, what was the point of being an anarchist if you are just going to play by a single set of rules.

Over the coming months, we got to play with all sorts of great bands and the occasionally mediocre. Some became famous but many did not. We played with *UK Decay*, *The Mob*, *Brigandage*, *The Sisters of Mercy*, *Billy Bragg*, *The Sex Gang Children* and many more.

Often, you find you have chosen sides without knowing. The agency that ran the Lyceum was not entirely happy with what they considered a rival promotion invading their territory. They thought strictly in terms of money and business. They honestly thought the Anarcho-scene was a competing company getting rich by stealing money from their pockets.

Later, I was to discover there was an actual blacklist against people who played there. It's often said you are not paranoid if they really are out to get you. Most people's paranoia is based on a delusion that anyone actually gives a shit about what they do. When you actually make it onto their radar, the powers that be generally like to let you know.

After our first record came out, *The Damned* wanted us to play on a bill with them and the *Lords of the New Church*. One of the promoters told me we would never have gotten onto one of their bills had the *Damned* not asked for us by name.

What fun do they have rubbing your nose in the shit if you don't know they're doing the rubbing? Power is all about signing your sins.

FORTY-EIGHT
ADELAIDE, SOUTH AUSTRALIA, 1978

Having been thrown off of the tour had opened up a variety of new complications. There was still a gig on the Friday at a University and the *ABC* (Australia's equivalent to the *BBC*) were wanting us to play live on television as part of a current affairs show called the *7:30 Report*. I was confused how that worked because it was supposed to be a national program but we were in a different time zone than all the bigger cities.

It had been arranged that we would set up in front of the hotel swimming pool. There was a huge camera crew running wires in all directions. I saw the pool and saw the wires and quietly considered how badly this could turn out.

Unfortunately, Mark Taylor had had to bail because the *Psycho Surgeons* weren't banned and they still had to play the remaining pub gigs. The last thing he needed was to be associated with low life like us.

We managed to recruit the guitarist out of a local band called *The Accountants*. He had this *Sid Vicious* clone thing going so that was fair enough.

I spent all day training him up on the songs; about ten hours of constant practice. I was fairly determined not to fuck this up but 5 minutes before the broadcast, we were cut from the show out of a fear of a *"Bill Grundy* Style Incident". That was probably a fairly wise decision on their part. I doubt we could have been trusted on national television. We were, essentially, arseholes. I, for one, had absolutely no intention of being trusted on live national television.

You've never seen a union crew pack up so quickly.

FORTY-NINE

West Croydon, London, 1983

Suddenly, we found ourselves installed in Wickham Studios in West Croydon. This was a ridiculous place to record if you lived in Stoke Newington and travelled by public transport. But this is where the record company sent us and they were footing the bill.

Or rather, they weren't. According to the contract, they were lending us money to go into the studio and, when the time came, we would have to pay them back out of our royalties. But we didn't get a choice about what studio we used.

Additionally, we would be paying for a master tape that we mixed the final product onto but that tape would be the property of the record company. I really wanted to explain this to you because this was standard music business practice.

They lend you money to make something they keep but you pay for. This is how the world works.

We knew this and we understood this going in. Even without paying for legal advice we couldn't afford, I knew how to read. I explained to everyone that this was a rort but it was only for one EP. We all agreed this was the only way we were going to release anything and it was better to get something released than not have any record of what we had done. This, at least, would vindicate our existence.

I had been assigned with the task of collecting Jez and dragging him to the recording studio. It was a godawful morning start and I don't do mornings at the best of times (or any time, really). For me, there was only a seven in the morning if you stayed up to greet it.

I was living in Bayston Road and Jez lived about a kilometre north in Cazenove Road. Jez had promised to leave a key under the mat. So, the day began with me walking through London's winter cold.

I'd been in the middle of a protracted breakup with my girlfriend, Angie. She had just joined a band and started staying overnight at their place. I'll admit I wasn't exactly heartbroken. She'd been attempting to swallow down bottles of paracetamol and I'd had to reach down her throat to make her puke. You kind of lose respect for someone after the first few times.

But look, no matter how badly a relationship is going, you don't want to watch someone overdose on paracetamol. That's a shithouse, painful way to go. Besides, it was clearly for show. There was a mouthful of pills but not a whole lot of swallowing going on.

There had also recently been an adventure where she had ran straight into a glass door. That ended in a trip to Hackney Hospital and a shit ton of stitches.

I felt somewhat responsible for these events. If you didn't live inside my head, it might be difficult to differentiate between obsessive hyperfocus and delusional narcissism. The chief difference is, of course, the ability to empathise. Expressing that empathy might, however, prove difficult.

So, of course, when I went up to collect Jez, I found that she was in bed with him in what I can only imagine was some kind of bizarre self-destructive urge on both their parts. She seemed disappointed that I didn't explode in a violent temper and he seemed disappointed that, one way or another, I was going to drag him to the recording studio.

Jez's major concern seemed to be he would not be able to score drugs if I took him to Croydon. I was offering no alternative. We were catching the 73 bus to King's Cross, a tube to Brixton and who knows what bus into the middle of nowhere. It gave me cold turkey just thinking about it and I wasn't even using.

Not that Jez really had to worry. The record company had also assigned us with a producer who we would also be paying for. *Miki Dallon* had produced a number of hits in the nineteen sixties and was a close personal friend of Chris Youle, the man who owned the record company. Pay attention. This will turn around and bite me in the arse later.

Anyway, *Miki* made a phone call and was quite happy to have drugs bought in whilst he spent the next fourteen hours fucking around with drum sounds. His joining in with the gang's consumption didn't seem to improve his hearing.

Like a particularly annoying optometrist he flicked between

settings asking Ralph, the engineer, "does this one sound better or does that one?" For the life of me, I couldn't tell the difference between one snare thwack and another.

Just so you know, I was sober. Ralph and I were the only sober people in the room listening to the Hell of the Infinite snare thwacks.

Around nine at night, we laid down the backing tracks. I was given to understand this was largely a guide for laying down the drums and we'd re-record the rhythm guitar. Twenty minutes later, those tracks were laid and we were moving right along.

I said I was really unhappy with the guitar sound and I had wanted some distortion. The set up for the recording of the guitar had been achieved by dumping a mic across a clean amp and a five second check to ensure sound was coming through.

"No, that was great. We'll add some distortion in the mix."

When someone tells you this in an analogue studio, let me tell you this is absolute bullshit. And whilst no-one these days records in analogue, if I can offer you one piece of advice. It can never be fixed in the mix.

After the literal hours spent on the drum sound, everything else was rushed through in record time. At about two in the morning, we were packed off in a minicab and sent back to Stoke Newington.

As it turned out, the night was still young. Travelling through the City of London, we were pulled over by the police. They probably only pull over one car a night and, given the empty streets around Liverpool Station, we seemed to be the only car they'd seen all night.

Oh, what fun. I found myself enjoying the pleasures of a strip search that only ended after the policewoman had put on a rubber glove and played a lovely little game of cavity search. That's a real fucking icebreaker, that is. I'm told some people would have paid good money for it.

I then stood around naked on the cold stone floor whilst they examined my guitar. As you may remember, I had stuffed it full of toilet paper to stop it from feeding back. They spent a considerable amount of time pulling toilet paper out through the f hole.

Finally, with the sun coming up, I was released to catch the 149 bus home. It had been an interesting twenty-four hours but it wasn't over yet.

I had secured a ticket to a free pre-screening of "*The Evil Dead*" at the Scala Cinema in the morning and I wasn't going to miss that. It had been described as the ultimate experience in gruesome terror. Maybe it was my biography.

Sam Raimi was there and, after it was over, they fed us with devon and tomato sauce sandwiches on stale white bread. I consumed it greedily because it was the first food I'd eaten in days.

After this so-called lunch, they shot the TV ad for the film because they couldn't screen anything from the actual film apart from a few establishing shots. You can look that ad up on the internet with me following directions of, "*Eyes wider. Eyes wider. Now look away*".

I had been on quite a rollercoaster over the previous thirty-six hours. I went home and slept for eighteen hours. No drugs were involved in my collapse.

FIFTY

Adelaide, South Australia, 1978

The rich are not merely just the most boring of people, they are also the most bored. Interestingly, if you do something disreputable, they (or their children) become desperate to drag you into their homes. With all the press coverage, we suddenly found ourselves invited to spend time hanging out around one of the rich folks' pools.

For ease of reference, a *Chokito* is a combination chocolate bar brand, created and owned by *Nestlé*. The original bar consists of an ingot-shaped caramel fudge centre, with a coating of milk chocolate and crisped rice on the outside. There are circumstances where it might be mistaken for a lumpy human turd.

Filth would naturally be blamed for this atrocity just waiting to happen but I'm more likely to blame either Mark Taylor or Stan Armstrong of the *Psycho Surgeons* or perhaps a combination of both working in tandem. Over the years, both have tended to raise their cards during questioning in what an experienced Poker player might call a tell.

Regardless, it was *Filth* who were chased down the road by a belligerent elderly man who was naked except for his white dressing gown, his slippers and a rolled-up newspaper he swung in ire.

"Who shat in my Pool?" he cried. A new *Agatha Christie* mystery in the making. A startling vision that could traumatise many a child.

Later, I ran across my long-lost brother, not that I recognised him. A weirdo approached me and started questioning me about things it would have been impossible for anyone to know about. Before you ask, my brain often has trouble recognising people's faces, particularly when said people are somewhere they should not ought to be.

It's nothing personnel. It's kind of like facial dyslexia. Hell, these days I look in a mirror and barely recognise myself but that may come down to vanity and self-denial.

My brother drummed for a band charmingly called *the Dagoes*. This raised in me some interesting questions regarding nature and nurture. We'd barely seen each other in the last ten years and we both still ended up in punk rock bands. This was Australia. At the time, it was hardly like there was a punk band on every street corner.

When we reached the University, we figured there must have been some kind of mistake. Maybe, they'd taken us to the wrong room. Surely, we should be playing in a small out house or something. This room was big and it was full and these people had come to see us.

It wasn't even later on in the evening full. It was full at doors open half an hour before the opening act hit the stage. So, no pressure. No sound check. No worries.

Then the weirdest thing of all happened. We did not choke. We did not snatch defeat from the jaws of victory. We just flat out nailed it. The whole room erupted. The dance floor was insane. We hit song after song without drawing breath.

The set closed with a cover of "Search and Destroy." I always liked leaving the stage with the guitar feeding back against the amp in a defiant *"that's your lot"* gesture. This was both theatrical and practical as the beating I would lay down on a guitar in the final song of the set would usually leave the guitar beyond any hope of tuning.

Electronic tuners were hardly the omnipresent beast they are today. It was still common to use pitchpipes.

If a guitar was being stubborn about feeding back, I would tap the headstock gently across a corner of the speaker cabinet. The jarring tone of the bump would usually circle back into the amp and a wall of thick warm feedback would soon envelop the room. It was a move I had successfully pulled off a hundred times in the past.

That night, it didn't work. Perhaps I got carried away and perhaps it was the straw that broke the camel's back. The headstock cracked off of the neck. Apparently, it's a fairly common problem with Gibson style guitars. I have since repaired a number of head stock breaks and, if anything, the guitar was tougher afterwards.

At the time and in my ignorance, I just said this one is fucked. I finished the set by smashing an Aria flying V into several thousand pieces. It was not a light guitar. The body was heavy like a dining room table and I used a metal chain for a strap.

It took some serious effort to splinter that beast. When I had finished, the crowd seemed to rise as one to salvage souvenirs from the stage. I saw my brother retreat back off into the dark. He was wielding half of the guitar's headstock like a pair of brass knuckles; the machine heads protruding from between his fingers.

FIFTY-ONE
Hackney, London, 1983

It is a perceived universal truth that even the most beautiful and perfect of things will carry within itself the seeds its own destruction. The ugly and the profane just get to kick themselves to the kerb that little bit faster.

Richard North, of *Kick* fanzine fame, had gotten a job with the *NME* and we got word they wanted him to do an interview with us. I still imagined it was going to be some kind of little puff piece even when they dragged *Anton Corbijn* in to take photos. *Corbijn* was even shooting in colour which was kind of weird for the *NME*. At the time it was a black and white smudge rag guaranteed to leave ink on your hands but not the paper.

I leaned heavily into the anarchy and mysticism angle firstly because it interested me. Secondly, it was because I didn't want to discuss why the rest of the band were off somewhere else doing drugs.

The day before it hit the street, I heard a rumour that we got the cover. I told the record company but I was careful to add that I thought someone was probably taking the piss. This was because I was fairly certain that someone had to be taking the piss.

The first time I saw the offending cover was when I went to the dole office to sign on. Sitting behind the counter and beside the

Administrative Officer checking the appropriate paperwork to my claim was a folded copy of the *NME*. It was folded in a perfect way so as to allow me to look directly at myself.

Awkward.

It was at this moment that I realised I could be famous and still utterly fucking broke. This monolith they called the music industry could work me a hundred hours a week and not give me a penny. I'd just come off of two days putting records into cardboard sleaves just to be fucking helpful.

The record company put us into a rehearsal room for a week so we could tour and promote the record. I found myself turning up alone, sitting around for four hours playing the guitar and going home. There was all kinds of weird stuff floating around the periphery. Sion had been acting as our manager and he was living with Lisa. Lisa apparently went off on a drug binge with Jez and the fallout from that was a fucking mess.

I was mostly only happy when I got put in the back of a van, driven off to a mystery destination to play before being put back in the van. At least during this period, I could switch off, stop thinking and collapse into a burned-out state of catalepsy, curled up in a ball on the cold metal floor. Some people will tell you wild stories about the life of a touring rock band. I usually dreamt I was being buried alive in a coffin.

People tell me that had memories of seeing the band in places I can't even remember being in. I can remember being in Leeds but, every time I went there, there was so much fog that I never actually got to see it.

One of the perverse pleasures of headlining was getting to play an encore. The encore we tended to play was a version of the *Velvet Underground*'s "*Sister Ray*". We would literally play that until someone pulled the plug on us.

The EP had gone quite well, crashing into the NME independent charts at number 4. In Melody Maker it went to number 2. In Sounds, which that week was essentially basing its charts on sales at the very local Small Wonders shop, we crashed in at number one.

We were in the *Face* Magazine. We were in *Sounds* and *Zigzag* but I'd long given up reading about myself. We were drowning in interviews. There was a bizarre television show called "*South of Watford*" where we were getting interviewed by *Michael Moorcock* of all people. Strangers wanted to talk to me on the street and I have a complete aversion to talking to strange people on the street. My experience of talking to strange people on the street had, for the most part, ended extraordinarily badly.

Even the old women who lived on the opposite side of the road no longer crossed themselves in fear. Nor did they pray to the Lord. They didn't even attempt to flee in mortal terror.

"*Hey, look, Mildred! It's him off the telly!*"

When did I get so God damn cuddly?

But other reasons for this lack of commitment to a life in the public eye were beginning to bubble and brew. I began to consider the difference between art and a craft. The development of craft is certainly what you need to achieve popularity and there is nothing stopping you combining it with art but it is an uneasy balance. Craft demands you narrow your gaze and colour inside the lines but art is wild freedom. You can craft your art into something more palatable but there is temptation with craft to attempt to skip any risk and settle on cold perfection.

Art helps you develop yourself as a person. You examine yourself and the world around you. It allows you to grow.

Was being on the cover of a magazine making me a better person? Probably not. It may have at least provided me with a sense of worth and I had surely evolved beyond my recent life as street trash. Or had I? Had I just built a straw house to hide from the wolves and the wind? Could one bad day return me to the gutter?

Apart from these unpleasant brushes with some kind of celebrity status, there seemed no transformation in the real world. The distant howling continued to greet the moon and the evil of men continued to circle.

We went to a *Part 1* gig in a church hall near Tottenham. The night ended with men with axes smashing through the door. These guys weren't even skinheads. They were like full on National Front goons. I had held the back door closed as long as

I could whilst people and instruments were thrown into one of those ubiquitous white hire vans.

I ended up running towards the van's open backdoor as it started to drive off. Hot in pursuit were the axemen of the apocalypse. Arms reached out to grab me and drag me into the van followed by the scream to *"Hit It!"*

Did everything have to be like a goddamn movie?

FIFTY-TWO
The Simpson Desert, South Australia, 1978

In the hotel, it was time to wake up and leave. The problem was that the hotel did not want us to leave. The way they told it, our fans had run amok during the night causing thousands of dollars' worth of damages. The authorities had been informed.

Firstly, I was confused that we had fans and, secondly, I was disappointed that I'd slept through the riot. A financial settlement was eventually made that simply meant none of us would be getting paid. The strangest thing about the music industry is the many and varied ways it can find not to pay you.

The roads in the centre of Australia are amazing. Horizon to horizon there is this featureless landscape of red, iron rich soil. The horizon does not end in hills or mountains; it just extends forever. With endless runs of straight road without landmarks, speed ceases to have any real meaning.

Even the sky was cloudless. The postcard azure of the sky seemed to darken to black at the apex. You could almost imagine stars at midday.

The car's speedometer was jammed far above the 140-mph mark. Occasionally, we would approach a car heading in the opposite direction applying the same pedal to the metal insanity it required to cross the desert. It would appear as a dot. The dot would quickly grow and rocket past before retreating into the rear-view mirror.

If there had been a head on collision at that speed, there would have been nothing left. The cars would have literally passed through each other in a shower of atomised gore. I could almost imagine it. The perfect ending to a story full of nihilism, incompetence and opportunities missed.

I found myself dozing in the back seat. Soon, I was floating above the car in an experience I can only describe as astral projection. Whilst I remain unconvinced in an actual astral plane, I am more than a little familiar with what can be best described as lucid dreaming. When you wake up in a dream, it is not an experience you forget in a hurry.

It doesn't matter what the actual mechanism or physiology is. Even the unreal can still feel like it is real. That hunk of meat in our heads is a totally unreliable narrator. We make excuses for experiences and pretend things never happened and yet weirdness is always nipping at our heels. Is anything true?

When we all fall asleep, where do we go?

Above the car, I was fighting with Pete Tillman. I hadn't quite worked out why I was fighting him but, at that very moment, I knew the entire *Filth* thing was over.

FIFTY-THREE
Maida Vale, London, 1983

Just so you don't get the idea that everything in the music business involves unpleasantry, I'd like to just tell you about how wonderful it was to do a session for the *John Peel Show*. I suppose this was an unusual experience in that, rather than telling us what we could do, they listened to what we wanted to do and went out of their way to accommodate that.

Now, before you get too carried away, they might have called it a *John Peel* session but he wasn't actually there to meet and greet you. He was back at home in Suffolk getting ready for his nightly show.

Despite that, this was perhaps the first time we weren't treated like incompetent weirdos, unrealistic idiots or just plain street scum. And to what should really come as no surprise to anyone, we responded to this respectful treatment by acting totally professionally. We didn't sit around knocking back cider. We worked with common purpose and focus, determined to do our best. All the petty squabbles of band life were pushed to the side. Granting someone a little dignity really goes a long way in this life.

For me, this is the reason the John Peel session sounds infinitely better than the *Love Under Will* EP. After getting the backing track down, they let me wipe the guitar and replaces it with an amp sound pushed hard into distortion. When I wanted to add feedback, they let me push the amp to ten and swing the guitar around the room. They didn't say "You can't do that". They just placed microphones in the best place to catch the sound.

When I suggested that one of the songs could do with some bell sounds to emphasise the melody, two guys in white lab coats arrived out of nowhere carrying a celeste.

When we wanted a church bell sound at the end of "*Spit on your grave*", someone went out into the car park and borrowed some poor bugger's hub cap. Even more surprising was that all the basic tracks for the four songs were knocked off in about two hours including set up.

FIFTY-FOUR
Sydney, 1978

We got word that the Bondi Life Saver wanted to give us a residency when we returned to Sydney. The Life Saver (or the Wife Swapper as it was not so affectionally nicknamed) was the home of traditional Australian rock. Given its air of blokey machismo the "Wife Beater" may have been a better name. Apparently, our future in *"the business"* was virtually assured. But how extreme would our circus have to be to satisfy the expectations and the hype?

"If I could stick a knife in my heart. Suicide right on stage. Would it be enough for your teenage lust? Would it help to ease the pain?"

Essentially, a monster had been created and the only way that monster could be delivered night after night was to turn the monster into show business. Once you do that, it is no longer a monster.

Nihilism cannot be maintained indefinitely; it wears you down. The recognition of meaninglessness creates the denial of meaning. At its heart is the dull pull of entropy. It demands that electrons slow and halt around the nuclei and temperatures drop to absolute zero. The complete opposite of Punk Rock.

How many times can you dive on broken glass until the scars and scabs out number clean flesh? When do you stop being you and become the injury?

How many times can you put the chain guitar strap over the cut it reopened the night before without infection and necrosis? How long can you keep on destroying without creating?

Filth didn't record a note in a studio. Someone shot a short film that, after one screening at Sydney University, vanished into a vault somewhere; never to be seen again. Some silent super 8 film of the gig at North Sydney appeared on a CD Rom attached to a punk compilation.

Someone set up a multitrack recorder at the Adelaide University gig. Apparently, these tapes were lost forever.

A bootleg tape of earlier performances appeared for a while but seemed to have been recorded on a cassette player running low on batteries. It contained performances from Lismore and the Baptism of Blood. The bootleg tapes run off the master were maybe two or three semitones sharp and were essentially unlistenable.

And maybe this is all for the best. What has more power; the legend or the reality? When I lived in Wollongong, *Channel Ten* was almost impossible to tune into. When the clouds were in the right places it would half emerge from the snow of static.

Channel Ten showed a lot of horror movies and I would stare at the screen trying to make out the story through the interference. Many of these films are more firmly implanted in my brain than anything seen clearly.

I left *Filth* because *Filth* had made itself completely and utterly redundant. We could not continue to play and live up to the stories we had created. Audiences would always expect a death trip and would only be disappointed by an entirely adequate punk band.

Besides, when Pete had said he wanted to be in a band like the *Psycho Surgeons*, what he really meant to say was he wanted to be in the *Psycho Surgeons*. His work in the *Lipstick Killers* pretty much proved his instincts were dead on the money.

But I still think the main problem was that we had somehow turned into a real band without really trying. We should have stuck with Noel.

FIFTY-FIVE
New Cross, London, 1983

After a brief period where I lived in Cross Street, Islington with the Black Sheep Housing Co-operative, I took up residence south of the river in New Cross with Mouse. Moving to New Cross was interesting as very few people from North London ever wanted to visit. Despite our proximity to the Underground Station, it was like having moved in to an entirely different world.

The houses of Nettleton Road had basically been handed over to a housing co-operative because of bomb damage during the war. On 25 November 1944, a V-2 rocket exploded at the nearby Woolworths store in New Cross Road. 168 people were killed, and 121 were seriously injured. The targeting of the docks and factories meant many bombs had been dropped in the surrounding area. The area between New Cross Gate Station and Surrey Quays was just rail lines and wastelands.

In the land to the west of Nettleton Road, a large bomb or rocket had dropped and the compression wave lifted the roofs off the houses before dropping them back in place.

This apparently rendered the houses uninhabitable for normal people (but all the buildings are still there today). One of the big things the bomb did was it cleared the land beyond the back yards and, essentially, a small forest had grown. Despite its Inner-City location, it almost felt kind of rural.

We often saw foxes and, on one memorable occasion, I had to do battle with a huge black rat much larger than any of our three cats. There had been a hissing around a curtain and suddenly all the cats turned and ran for their lives. This thing was fucking huge with evil black eyes. It backed itself into a corner and leapt at anyone who approached it.

When I say leapt, it was heading up to crotch level. You certainly didn't want that thing latching on to any part of your anatomy. Everyone fled the kitchen except Mouse and I. I finally knocked it out of mid-air with a hammer. The sense of victory was weird, an adrenaline rush that edged towards nausea. But, seriously, no-one was ever going to go to sleep with that thing loose in the house.

Nettleton Road was a busy little artistic hub all of its own. There was *Test Department* and the *Band of Holy Joy* as well as members of *Hagar the Womb*. The comedian *Vic Reeves* also lived there. Apart from when Millwall played home games at the Den, it was far calmer and more peaceful than anywhere I'd lived previously in London.

On days when Millwall did play at home, buses and cars were overturned and set on fire. Police on horseback would battle hooligans, truncheons drawn. Helicopters flew overhead as streets were sealed off and rows of police vehicles parked behind the barricades.

Yes, it could get a little over the top but it also had a quiet predictability and the violence, for once, wasn't about you. You could still walk around and go shopping unmolested if you weren't flying football colours.

For me, there was the added advantage that I was far from Stoke Newington and no longer my brother's keeper. Speaking of whom, we had a gig in Brighton and Jez was absolutely nowhere to be found. His involvement with and endless hustle for heroin had become unsustainable. His bad days had become bad weeks and his bad weeks had become bad months. And there's some stuff you just can't talk people out of. You have to let them hit bottom.

Lisa said we could always collect Ralph on the way through Croydon and it was about that stage I realised they were going to make a cute couple. I'm guessing there had been a plan cooking whilst I was away in the South. Almost as quickly as he had arrived, Jez was out on his arse. You could do drugs. You could miss rehearsals. But you didn't miss gigs or photoshoots.

Ralph would go on to become a successful record producer. He would, amongst many others, produce *EMF*'s *"You're Unbelievable"* single. It seems odd that anyone who would ever amount to anything actually became involved with us.

I taught him the whole set in the back of the van as we puttered slowly south on the A23. We played in an underground cellar and certainly sounded better than we had with Jez.

At the end of the night, I watched a kid who had been to the gig frolicking away from the venue through a park. He was decked out in a full vampire cape and pirouetted around benches, obliviously happy.

I mention it now because I had never previously considered that our music could make people happy. We were such a bunch of dark clouds.

We wandered down and sat on the smooth pebbles that the residents of East Sussex seemed to think of as a beach. The waves lapped gently onto the stones. Beyond the reach of the street lights the world was totally black.

It wasn't just the band there. There were quite a few people we knew who had all travelled down for a good time by the sea. It was a lovely group of people and, for the first time in a long time, I felt comfortable in myself. I didn't have to be anyone. There were no imminent threats and no sense of pressure. I could almost believe that things would be okay. If this could be my life, I could be perfectly happy with it.

But I'm always unrealistic. If you can't make trouble for yourself, someone is bound to make it for you.

FIFTY-SIX
Sydney, 1978

If you had seen a photo of me in those days, you could not fail to notice that I was impossibly skinny. I didn't smoke, I didn't drink and I didn't do drugs but I still looked like I had been freed from a concentration camp.

It wasn't like I wasn't eating. I must have eaten a hamburger every day and, if I didn't, I made sure I at least ate a bread roll. And I made sure to take a multi-vitamin tablet too. After all, you have got to look after yourself.

I had to admit that I wasn't feeling great and so I went to see a doctor. With my usual sense of optimism, I expected cancer. His diagnosis was malnutrition but he wasn't entirely sure because he had never actually seen a case. He'd seen pictures in text books but this was modern day Sydney. The only people who starved in Sydney were the metho drinking dossers.

In Francis Street, opposite the *Villa de Filth*, there was a corner store that kept mentholated spirits in the refrigerator next to the milk and the cokes. Skeletal men would emerge from boarding houses, collect a bottle and try to die in Hyde Park.

With the benefit of hindsight, I'm considering I may have been suffering from some kind of a reaction to trauma. There was all the not eating and self-harm and stuff.

But I can't just blame simple things like trauma. There were also the records and the gigs and these were such a source of comfort and joy that food was more a secondary concern. There were just so many punk records coming out in 1977 and 1978 that it was hard to keep up. From a time of cultural famine, a great abundance had grown. From every corner of the world came the new.

It also seemed like if you didn't get them when you saw them, they vanished; never to be seen again. When I eventually left Sydney, I would sell all my records at a market stall in Paddington. If I still had them all, Discogs suggests I could probably, at the very least afford a smallish mansion overlooking the sea. But I'm not the kind of person who thinks in terms of speculation.

Is pop a pleasure best left ephemeral? The passion to catch the moment is an addiction as profound as any drug.

FIFTY-SEVEN
Marylebone, London, 1983

Chris Youle, head honcho of *Kamera Records*, was in his cups. His sorrows needed a quick dipping. Despite having *the Au Pairs* and *The Fall* on his label, royalties would soon need to be paid and do you really need me to explain what that means.

He had the Receiver on speed dial and an open invitation to bankruptcy court. Tired and emotional, he talked to me paternally (if your father was the living incarnation of Satan). "*I hate it when a girl wants to kiss you after she's sucked your dick. Especially if you've just screwed her up the arse.*"

A and R man, Saul Galpern burped loudly. It was as close as he could manage to a laugh. He proceeded to detail an industry junket in Paris he had attended with Mister Youle. He was especially proud of the fact that the pair had managed to split up a boy-girl pop duo that had a string of number ones under their belts. Given that this is the early nineteen eighties and I've been reminded of libel laws, you'll have to guess the name of these Top of the Poppers without additional clues.

The way Saul told it, he and Youle hired a prostitute to pass the male member a nice dose of Herpes. This, they thought, would break up the pair both professionally and romantically. This surprised me on two levels.

Firstly, I (as well as a large proportion of the record buying public) had assumed the bleached blond male was not exactly interested in female company. I have, however, been known to be wrong about these things.

Secondly, it seemed fairly unlikely that this pair of idiots could organise the purchase of a pair of plane tickets, let alone bring the intricate details of this cunning Machiavellian plan to fruition. Besides, this would have required finance as well as finesse. It was true these men had deep pockets but they were cursed with undeniably short arms.

Both Chris and Saul were laughing very loudly at this point of the story. They patted each other's backs and raised glasses in triumph. This was clearly a story that improved with every retelling.

Probably more through luck than design, this duo had indeed split up and, failing to find any kind of solo success, I guess both went back to riding the till at the local Sainsburys or cutting hair in a boutique in Croydon.

Whilst you know this whole story strikes me as fairly unlikely, I include it here to demonstrate the high moral qualities and intellectual prowess possessed by the people on the business side of the industry. The whole system runs on a healthy diet of urban myth, ridiculous scheming and downright delusion.

As sure as night follows day, the financial year turned and *Kamera Records* shuttered their doors, the contents of their office vanishing overnight. It was almost as if they had never been there at all.

The rights and ownership of all materials related to *Blood and Roses* quietly passed into the hands of Chris' good friend *Miki Dallon*. They would occasionally find re-issue through bizarrely curated releases in overseas markets with covers splashed in garish neon colours and the words "*New Wave*" plastered in the largest font available.

It would be embarrassing to be swindled by men such as these if you hadn't seen it coming. All confidence tricks involve belief in a dream; the impossible made possible. The notion that our art was worthwhile makes us all seem gullible. But, as I've said, I had read the contract and looked at the numbers and knew we'd never get rich digging this particular ditch.

Broke and with no label to call home, some overly positive soul suggested there was nowhere else to go but up. The music press lost interest and offers of gigs began to dry up.

There had been plans to play an all-nighter at the *Scala* cinema in Kings Cross. It had been a suggestion I had made largely based on history. Back in the seventies, *Lou Reed* and *Iggy and the Stooges* had played there. If you ever went there, you could recognise the barrier *Iggy* was climbing over on the back cover of *Raw Power*.

Unfortunately, a neighbouring gambling hall took offence at the noise we made during the sound check and demanded we desist. I had finally reached the stage in what I laughing call a career where I was actually being paid not to play.

Or, to be more precise, *"Take this and fuck off before we break your legs."*

FIFTY-EIGHT
Haymarket, Sydney, 1978

In a world where guitarists outnumber useful musicians by about a five to one ratio, being a guitarist without a guitar is not going to help your career trajectory. So, I'm doing an office job that's pulling in a bit over $120 a week. Rent is $18 and I walk everywhere. I figure that, on one hamburger a day, I can probably spend $85 on a guitar.

The doctor had told me that this kind of diet would kill me but he had prescribed me a bottle of a revolting iron supplement. It tasted like an old man had vomited blood on dog shit. Or at least, it made me imagine what old man's blood on dog shit would taste like.

Anything that foul I figured must be doing something good for me. This was a time before strawberry flavouring when medicines were expected to taste bad to prove they actually worked. This stuff tasted so bad that I was expecting to develop spider senses and super powers.

Well, I wasn't going to be able to afford anything out of one of those posh guitar shops. You could buy cheap electric guitars in places like K-mart but they were unplayable with cheese grater action and electronics that sounded awful. They were the kind of guitars kids would throw their dreams and their hard-earned Saturday job dollars at only to find an instrument with an inherent unplayability that would render their dream impossible.

Real guitar shops had pretty decent Japanese guitars next to their Gibsons and Fenders but they had new guitar prices. I was looking for something a junkie would trade in for a fix. Sometimes, you just have to use the cruelty of the music business to your advantage. And, let's face it, most of us would be selling guitars for a fix sooner or later. What goes around comes around.

So, there's this beautiful Aria Diamond guitar in the window of a second-hand shop in Elizabeth Street. It's basically the shape of *Johnny Ramones'* Mosrite except it was in sunburst. Compared to the Flying V I'd been dragging around; it weighed exactly nothing. The neck was thin and the action incredibly low.

It was desperate to play punk rock. I could tell. Charlie Hellcat had taught me how to do *Johnny Thunders* bends on the Adelaide tour. This guitar just loved them. It stayed in tune no matter how much I fucked with the G string.

And there was the price tag; $85.

Cold hard cash hit the counter and the guitar joined the *Urban Guerillas*. Oh, the places it would go; the harsh treatment it would receive.

FIFTY-NINE
Home Counties Death March, 1983

Ralph was still working at Wickham Studios and this gave us some dead time to record demos. We tried shopping them around and, although they sounded good, no-one was interested. We visited record companies big and small. They'd invite us in and call in the cleaners to disinfect the place when we left.

We largely found ourselves doing benefit shows where we essentially charged the cost of renting the van and we could keep that up for just about as long as we kept getting those expenses. We weren't selling merchandise or making any money. We were merely battling to keep the show on the road. If someone defaulted on payment, I found myself in the role of being the guy who stuck someone's head down the toilet until money rolled out of their pockets.

This was not a role I relished but the rest of the band were demanding gigs that paid money and we weren't getting any. To keep the band going, I was taking anything. But if it meant we were losing money, the whole thing was going to fall apart. I had to be the heavy. I probably wasn't the best choice for the heavy but I was most desperate to keep the show on the road.

And, of course, the rest of the band wanted money. They were supporting rapidly growing habits. I was just hanging on to an ideology and the desire to make music. I don't know which of these addictions was worse. Both led to the same downward spiral and that spiral continued into a godawful blur.

I had been used to perceiving time in terms of past, present and future. Reality had flattened into an endless dreary now. We were mice on a treadmill and lived in a constant state of putting one step ahead of another.

We did a CND benefit in St Albans. A crop headed gronk climbed up on stage and started groping Lisa. I belted him baseball bat style into the fifth row with my guitar and suddenly half a dozen of his fellow gronks climbed onto the stage and pretty much steamrollered me. I came to on the floor a metre and a half below and behind the stage. I had flown through the air with the greatest of ease but had no knowledge of doing so.

The neck of my guitar had broken in the fall and I had to drive a screw from neck through to body in order to continue.

Everything finally came to a head at a polytechnic gig. Richard had taken it upon himself to steal one of the support bands amps. I was in the front of the van and didn't know anything about it. By the time I received a request for it to be returned, my investigations revealed it had vanished up Richard's arm.

It was over. I was done. Flogging a dead horse was one thing but saying it smelled of roses was another. Worst of all, I hated having to lie.

Nothing keeps you going more than thinking you are fighting the good fight. This was no longer the good fight. This was rabid dogs eating rabid dogs. I climbed out of the pit and left them to it.

I took a job in a comic shop.

SIXTY

Darlinghurst, Sydney, 1978

Sometimes, you form a band because you are a bunch of friends hanging out and you are bored and you like a certain kind of music. Sometimes you just want to form a band and you recruit whoever the hell you can to fill the necessary pieces.

I think almost all the best bands form out of a clean and clear vision. You set up parameters you are going to work within. You start with a manifesto and you recruit around that manifesto. You will divert over time but your purity at the beginning makes it easier to drag life, kicking and screaming, into reality.

At work, I hung one picture beside my desk, an iconic image clipped from a newspaper. Patty Hearst's FBI wanted photo in front of the SLA flag, semi-automatic in hand and beret on head. This very much represented the visual aesthetic I thought this new band should have.

Okay, we weren't going to be robbing any banks but I thought suggesting we might be entirely capable of robbing banks was something we could float out into the wider world. Not so much dope, rock and roll and fucking in the street as a dedicated push for positive change. The band politics would be further left than Labor party left. We would unashamedly voice our position. There would be no songs about cars or girls or hamburgers sizzling on an open grill.

We would be proud commie anarchist rat bags.

Dressing like Patty Hearst was fairly straight forward too. With the Vietnam War over, the city had a string of army surplus stores stacked floor to roof in jungle green. Everyone wore ex-army clothes because they were dirt cheap and they didn't fall apart after half an hour.

We were to become the *Urban Guerillas*. Another band with that name would emerge from South Australia about a year later and they're still going to this day. They're nice enough guys with a left-wing lean. They put out records. I've got no problem with them. I'm just making sure you know that this was a very different band to them.

I consider our version of the *Urban Guerillas* as being an important and unique Australian band despite being nearly forgotten and I don't say that lightly. We were genuinely and effortlessly our own one of a kind of thing.

Lyrically, we probably floated more towards the *Clash*. I had plenty of songs from *Filth* in my pocket and many just needed a brush up of lyrics. I've never had a problem changing lyrics because the meaning of words changes quickly. What is (for want of a better term) politically correct at one point of time can quickly become offensive in another time. Historically, words are not nailed to their meaning.

Some people tell you the original lyrics are the genuine thing and sacrosanct. They'll tell you changing words is like screwing with the Bible. Singers particularly feel this way because they don't want to learn new lyrics.

My golden rule is, if I wouldn't write a particular line today, that line has to go. Just imagine a friend taking offence and let it go. And language is such a fluid thing. To change it is to remain relevant.

Songs like Patti Smith's *Rock and Roll Nigger* or John Lennon's *Woman is the nigger of the world* certainly had entirely different cultural baggage fifty years ago. No white artist in their right mind would evoke these as concepts as acceptable in the modern world. So, change is good.

A number of comedians will complain about wokeness. They remember a time they could put on a dress and get a laugh. But even they know if they get up on stage with a routine of Sixties' variety show gags, they're going to fall flat on their wrinkled faces.

Musically, it was also really important for us to play tight. We had something to say and we didn't want to make a joke out of it by fucking up. You know that equal and opposite reaction thing in physics? I was coming off being in *Filth*. Feedback would still play its part but the frame work was going to be solid.

Once instance proved how serious this rule was. We had a song called *"End of the Western World"* which started with a drum roll. At one rehearsal, Peter, the original drummer, deliberately started by copying the failed drum roll from the *"Live at the Roxy*

Album" version of *X-Ray Spex* song "*Oh Bondage, Up yours*."

Upon hearing the sound of toms falling down the stairs, I pulled the song up.

"*We won't be doing that,*" I said.

"*But,*" he replied. "*When they play it, it's funny and it's cool.*"

"*No, it isn't,*" I insisted. "*That was a mistake they made. When they recorded the single, that did not play that fucked up drum roll. We are not going to have fucked up drum rolls.*"

We restarted the song and obviously he had been practicing this dumb fucked up roll. He played it exactly the same again. I pulled the song up again.

"*We are not fucking doing that,*" I explained. "*And if you do that again, I will fucking kill you.*"

Everybody else in the room could see I was serious. Insane, maybe. Lacking a sense of humour, definitely. But we were paying money for a rehearsal studio; money none of us had.

He did it again with a soppy great smirk across his face. Without hesitation, I dived over the drum kit with every intention of committing homicide.

Unsurprisingly, Peter Macgregor was out of the band.

Somewhere in the Bible it says *"I will spit you out of my mouth because you are only warm and not hot or cold."* Punk rock was a lot like that.

SIXTY-ONE
New Cross, London, 1984

And so began the quite times. New ideas were forming in my head, they were bubbling out of my head but, I was so unwanted, I couldn't get arrested if I walked down the street naked with a gun.

I put bands together like the doomed but personally beloved Сексмйссйя. I did solo stuff. I just couldn't make it stick. Of course, a large part of that came down to my inability to shake hands, do small talk and smile in any of the right places. I couldn't walk up to strangers. I couldn't sell myself.

I realised that I had always used others to sell me and what I wanted to do. I hated to admit it but it was an excellent strategy because it bypassed all my biggest weaknesses as a human being.

I often saw people who could do it effortlessly. They either put on a mask or, more terrifyingly, maybe they really were always that narcissistic and shallow. I remember seeing *Kirk Brandon* (later to be of *Theatre of Hate*) work a tube train from one end to another, glad-handing as he promoted his bottom of the bill performance with *The Pack* at the Lyceum.

The thing is, I couldn't imagine doing that. That would be humiliating. I hate people who do that. I'd have to beat myself up if I did that.

So, it boils down to this. Is it the doing of something that is important or is it the acknowledgement you receive for doing something. I had brushed up against success enough to know that I didn't particularly like it. It meant brushing up against humans and, whilst I quite enjoy talking to individual humans, as a species they disturb me.

I did like performing and creating but I was beginning to realise that what you gave an audience was enough. You did not particularly need to get anything back. You make something up in your head, you deliver it into the world but you don't need a thank you note or a pat on the back. You need to learn to be happy just to get the stupid thing out of your head.

My relationship with Mouse broke down as she became increasingly involved with *Psychic TV*. She was off to Japan doing proper rock star stuff and wanted to pursue a more interesting life than me. I'd had interesting up to my eyeballs.

Genesis and crew kept turning up for sit down formal dinners and I was way too autistic to deal with that kind of shit. I was probably a bit of an embarrassment because I still had an unwavering conviction that family dinner equated to human sacrifice. That had been my general experience throughout childhood.

Small talk was something I just didn't get how to do on the best of days. Anyway, it was better for Mouse. She could go off and have adventures of her own.

I was kind of happily in the mood to fall off the face of the earth. I did get to play in a spin off support band for *Psychic TV* at Stoke Newington Town Hall with Mouse and Paula.

I got to make hideous feedback and noise for about half an hour which is one of the things I still enjoy doing. It was a rare opportunity to perform it for an audience that actually wanted feedback and horrible noise.

I also got invited to various recording sessions for what was supposed to be *Psychic TV*'s third album. I took that as an excellent learning opportunity because they were prepared to break every rule in the studio book. They'd been playing a song live called *Southern Comfort* and it did steer a little close to plagiarism of *Ry Cooder*'s soundtrack from the *Walter Hill* film.

The take they had done was really good but they weren't entirely happy because it sounded too obvious. So, they flipped the two-inch tape over so the entire backing track was playing in reverse and then started overdubbing on top of that.

I stored all I saw in the back of my mind. Not so much the exact details but the attitude. The idea that a recording studio was more than a place to capture a moment; the recording studio was an instrument that could be played. It could contribute to the process. In many ways, watching this process was inspirational for the recording of the *Blood and Roses* album.

There were other odd gigs here or there and the occasional bit of bad behaviour. Okay, there was a fair bit of bad behaviour at that support gig for the *Subhumans* at Stratford. In my defence, I saw this guy being hassled by security and I wanted him left alone because, you kind of want to be protecting the audience even when they got a little out of hand. It's a punk rock standard.

Unfortunately, when he was returned to the audience and started beating people up, I did feel it had become my responsibility to kick the living shit out of him because now security was no longer going to deal with him. I had, once again, become my brother's keeper and my brother had earned an arse-whooping.

To live in this world, it was clear I would need to make some kind of reassessment. Impulse control was not my strong suit and I had to learn that my side quests for justice may have needed a greater observation of the facts.

Though I tried not to be, there was a fair chance that - on top of everything else – I might just be an arsehole. But, ultimately, isn't everybody?

SIXTY-TWO
Brisbane, Queensland, 1978

I have always considered cover versions useful particularly when you are starting a band. You can have great originals and you can do a set of great originals but it can leave an audience detached. Until they have learnt your songs, they have little to grasp on to.

Even when the audience thinks they grasp your meaning, they may have grasped the entirely wrong end of the stick. If you can't clue them in, they may have no indication of what you are doing. They need a few hints.

At one gig, a young man came up to me to tell me how much he loved the masturbation song. I was surprised. To my knowledge, I had not written a song about masturbation and there was nothing about our stage presence that suggested the act of masturbation. Call me a prude, but I didn't really want to write songs about masturbation.

Perhaps he thought we were a bunch of wankers. I know. But it's better for me to pick up the low hanging fruit rather than leave it to someone else to make the overly obvious joke.

I asked him to sing the song and I immediately recognised it. I told him the chorus wasn't "Masturbation". It was *Smash your TV*. He refused to believe me, thinking I was winding him up. He knew what he'd heard and he knew what he liked. "Masturbation" was his anthem.

Cover versions do more than give an audience a touch of familiarity. They offer a context and help them get a handle on what you are doing. The *Urban Guerillas* made rules about covers. A lot of bands were peppering their sets with British Punk Songs and the scene around the Grand Hotel was becoming very much recognised as being derivative of the UK.

Our first rule was a cover version couldn't come from a band that was still playing. We played covers by The *Sonics*, The *Stooges*, The *Dolls*, The *MC5* and the *Alice Cooper Band*. We initially operated under a regime of two originals and one cover. The covers began to edge out as our own material became more recognised by the crowd.

Our first gig was in Brisbane. We stayed at *Razar*'s house. The band hadn't really settled on a line up and there was some question about the original singer's mental health. The tour began with a drunken overnight train trip. We were only asked once to calm down or we'd be thrown off the train. We'd been drinking all night with the conductor and she finally decided it was time we all calmed down. Like good children, we all went off to our seats to sleep.

I was fairly used to receiving police interest in Sydney. They'd pull you over, search you and rough you up. They'd let you go. Then you'd walk half a mile down the road and the same cops would pull you over and repeat the process. It was the cost of doing business, the business being living.

Brisbane cops were the next level up. They put the fascist into the regime. The footpaths had white lines and, if you stepped on the wrong side, they could pull you in. If you walked around in groups of more than two, the cops could bring you in. If they didn't like the look of you, they dragged you in.

If the cops dragged you in, they took all your money and threw you back out on the street. And the cops were huge. Sydney cops looked like they played on a rugby team. Brisbane cops looked like they lived in the gorilla enclosure at Taronga Park Zoo.

There were also plain clothed cops dressed as hippies sent to infiltrate gigs and parties. We got one drunk and gave him a punk haircut. That's when we found out he was an undercover cop because his mates burst in to save him.

After about twelve hours, I was already planning how to assassinate Joh Bjelke-Petersen who was the state's Ober Fuhrer. There seemed to be an inordinate number of rifles in the house. It was not something you saw in Sydney. More oddly still, when the cops raided the house, they were entirely disinterested in the guns.

On return, we'd pretty much decided to recruit Andi as our singer. Simplistically, if we were going to invoke an image of Patty Hurst, a woman singer went a long way to building that image. But the choice was built on so much more than that. She had the absolute presence to front a band and the band could just concentrate on being the band behind her.

As a wider audience began to arrive from the outer suburbs,

testosterone was on the rise. Too many people were coming in with a perception of punk as being simple, macho and stupid fun. The art of it was being pushed aside. There were people who thought the Ramones were serious. They just bought into the joke.

I think we'd all pretty much decided that the best way a punk band could develop was to not be a boy's club. Having a woman sing who wasn't going to lean into a femme fatale dynamic was even better.

In terms of the Sydney punk scene, I cannot tell you how revolutionary this idea was. Andi deserves to be an icon but the uber masculinity that still swamps the scene will always do their best to ignore her contribution.

SIXTY-THREE
New Cross, London, 1985

Then, out of the blue, Lisa and Ralph approached me about recording a *Blood and Roses* album. Ralph, through his work at Wickham Studios, had had some contact with Backs Records in Norwich and they were apparently keen.

I had but one question. "Is Richard going to be involved?"

I repeated the question several times. I didn't want to roll up and find that they just hadn't been able to find another drummer and dragged him back at the last moment. Although I had pretty much buried the hatchet on a personal level, band level is something different.

If you've set a moral and political model for your band, you can't just side step it for opportunity. Most successful bands will say this kind of thinking is naïve but I live in my head and it's hard enough being in there without dirtying the place up more than I have to.

Ralph assured me that he had a drummer and Richard would not be involved. It seemed they had already worked out what my possible objections would be and they had taken them into consideration. I may be a weirdo with stupid ideas but at least I'm kind of an open book weirdo.

In the years that had passed, Jez had gone into rehab. He came out, got drunk and died being run over by a bus. (As a side note; Noel from *Filth* had also died being run over by a bus. Losing one ex-band member in such a particularly specific and unusual manner might be considered unfortunate...)

On the *Love Under Will* EP, Jez had done all the keyboards because he had actually learnt how to play the piano. His playing on the long version of *Necromantra* was an unexpected highlight of those recordings. There had been a grand piano in the studio and we just kind of tried it out because it was there. Realising how important a part keyboards would play on the album, I immediately set to work in learning how to at least play one note melody lines and a few chords.

Fortunately, there was an old grand piano at Nettleton Road. It hadn't been tuned in about a hundred years but it was close enough in tune for jazz. I forced my clumsy hands to at least appear confident and competent.

I literally burned some midnight oil. Over the next few weeks, I created a pile of sheet music in preparation, double and triple checking that all the lines were in the right key. Years earlier, I had felt embarrassed when an engineer pointed out a guitar lead line was in a major key whilst the chord was a minor. It was probably just a passing comment but it cut me to the quick. How could I have not noticed? I had become determined I would never make the same mistake again.

It is amazing how much humiliation pushes you to improve. In most forms of art, they talk about professionalism without a clear standard you have to achieve. It is easy to feel like an imposter.

In preparation for the album, I strained my brain with paperwork. It was the last time I ever did so. When I arrived at the studio, Ralph asked me what that was for. He explained to me that no-one ever read that musical note shit. And I suddenly realised, no-one in rock and roll actually did.

SIXTY-FOUR
Railway Square, Sydney, 1978

Names can be deceiving. When they opened the Grand Hotel on Railway Square, the owner probably envisioned olde world opulence with the great and the good joining up at the bar to toast their good fortunes and discuss matters of empire. It hadn't quite panned out that way. Behind the imposing façade of Victorian and Edwardian splendour, the décor was pure bargain basement. The walls were panelled in nicotine yellowed veneer and the fixtures kept to the barest of minimums. Dreams are one thing but paying for them is quite another. As the years rolled on, the place tumbled down hill until it finally became the home of Sydney Punk.

The front bar was scary enough for your more gentile drinker. That end of town had become the last preserve of the old-time union labourer. There were brewers and printers and Darling Harbour was still a working wharf in theory at least. Hard days at work meant a hard day's thirst but an easy day of bludging did not decrease the need for booze in the slightest. As the six o'clock swill rolled around, short squat men cultivated their future strokes, heart attacks and liver failures. Urban decay was in full bloom and gentrification was not a concept in anyone's vocabulary. Nah, mate. Rich people don't want to hang around here.

The back bar was where the bands played. I have heard people describe the trepidation they felt as they stumbled into that far from hallowed room. I don't know what the hell they were talking about. I was young and arrogant enough to treat the place like it was my living room. There was no place like home.

And why not? The publican rarely came back there unless the liquor license people were checking for underage drinkers. He had no interest in the music but let's give the devil his due. He didn't really give a shit about what was happening just so long as the beer kept pouring. Well, this was Australia, mate. The beer fucking rained down.

Initially, the venue was set up by *Johnny Dole and the Scabs* because no-one else would have them. The *Psycho Surgeons* played there as did *X*, *Rocks* and *News* (formerly the *Babeez*). The *Leftovers* kept coming down and threatening to play but, somehow, they always managed to prove their own worst enemies and failed to follow through. (And don't think I don't know who nicked my copy of *"Little Johnny Jewel"*.) *Fucking Leftovers!*

By late 1978, you'd have to have gone to the Grand if you wanted to see the *Urban Guerillas* and Andi and Ross from the band had kind of become defacto bookers. Most sane people didn't go there. Outfits like the *Scabs* and *Tommy and the Dipsticks*, *Blackrunner*, The *Last Words*, The *Thought Criminals* and *Shock Treatment* had pretty much become fixtures. But even the more Avant Garde stylings of *Volght 465* and the *Slugfuckers* found a stage.

We were the dregs that didn't fit in with any of the other scenes about town and thus found ourselves in the enviable position of drawing all the other dregs to our side. If you sat long enough in the Grand, every freak in Sydney would eventually stand before you. The place started pulling in crowds.

In the early days there had been maybe twenty or thirty punters on a Friday and Saturday night. By the end of 1978, the room was pulling 200 to 250 a night and this was not a massive room. The *Urban Guerillas* were no small part of this. Thursday night had been added and we were usually playing twice a week.

The great, the good and the really quite dreadful came to play. We all wailed horrible noise to greater or lesser adulation. This was a truly great time for music but a piss poor time for business. The industry hoped if they ignored us long enough, we'd all just go away and, for the most part, they were right.

The old guard were still chugging out recycled *Status Quo* riffs as if that was the ultimate school of cool. Left deaf to criticism by walls of Marshall amps, they continued to haunt the beer barns that proliferated at city's edge. Some, like the *Angels*, *Midnight Oil* and *Mi-Sex* attempted to wrap their old school tat in the New Wave Emperor's new clothes. Some of them even made a career out of it.

Meanwhile, the original new wavers looked down their noses and claimed we either ripped off their thunder or diluted the purity of their vision. These were the style captains of the Inner-City Sound and had feathered the best roosts. Disavowed by both sides, we had nowhere left to go except the Grand.

It was a Thursday night when I fell in love *and when I say I'm in love you best believe I'm in love. L. U. V.* We had just slammed our way through a cover of the *Doll*'s *Looking for a Kiss* when I caught sight of her green hair. Okay. I tell a lie. We were actually playing *Search and Destroy* but you have to allow me a little bit of literary licence. We had knocked the Doll's song out earlier in the set so it wasn't a total lie.

Don't worry. I'm laying the ironies and the coincidences out in plain sight so that they don't come as a surprise later. It's just a simple matter of rearranging history in the search of a greater truth. What? Haven't you ever read a Hollywood script?

You can easily make two characters one. You can change the order of events. You can make something that happened there happen here. For fuck's sake, I've done it throughout this entire book. The story is more important than the details. Real life just gets in your face and makes no sense to anyone. It's all just one long, "*What the fuck was that?*"

You have to inject some order in to your "*what I did in the school holidays*" essay. You can't rely on an endless parade of "*and then*", "*and then*" and "*then*."

Stories are much better at telling the truth than the truth. And, if you can say it's only a story, you have so much more freedom to tell the actual truth. When the accusations and cries for justice come flying in, you can say it was only a story.

SIXTY-FIVE
West Croydon, London, 1985

The world is fickle. The things we are the most passionate about and most proud of may not be what the world wants or needs. We were very passionate about the *Enough is Never Enough* LP. In the opinion of many, the *Love Under Will* EP was great and this new thing was some kind of treacherous abomination.

We collectively despised the weedy sound of the EP and all the compromises we had to make to do it. We wanted an LP that sounded like the *Peel* sessions. Even after thirty years, listening back at it, I would have only done two things differently.

We recorded *Tomorrow* at the speed we played it live. In hindsight, it could have been a touch slower. And *Roles* should have had a big bright acoustic guitar in the mix. That is minor complaints for anything you create. Your inner critic can procrastinate forever if you let the little bugger loose.

The album was recorded quickly, too. We certainly didn't have a massive budget. We recorded in dead time, usually late night to early morning. Some of the sessions ran for thirty-six hours straight. We used second (more like fiftieth) hand two-inch tapes. There was no hire gear and all travel was by train or bus. I even got the Marshall amp down there on public transport.

We did a little fucking around in advance recording the *Theme from Escape from New York* which ended up as a B-side. That was only done so I could learn to program a drum machine and how to work the synthesizer. We knocked that out in a couple of hours.

There are certain things I believe you need to create art but ultimately all these things are disposable. You should have a concept, a sense of what you are doing and why you are doing it. A blank canvas is pure, perfect and clean. You should really have more of a reason to defile it with paint than mere expression of ego.

The third requirement is planning; ensuring you have the resources, skills and tools to bring your vision to life. You've got to let that big idea roll obsessively around in your head, contemplating variation and questioning decisions.

The fourth is having the will to pull it off because the world will do whatever it can to distract you, disenfranchise you or just make you doubt yourself.

Finally, you need the magic fairy dust of improvisation because, when all your best laid plans turn to shit, you had better be able to fix things on the fly. And your plans will turn to shit because, when you're broke, there's no place for contingency.

We had been very much a guitar-based band and it was important to retain that. Eight of the songs had played a large part in the sets we had been playing and that was the rock we built on.

.

Enough is Never Enough and *Whirr* were both about stepping completely out of that template and going as far as we could whilst still retaining the band's atmosphere. *Some Like It Hot* was about stepping as deep as we could inside the template and wrestling out what we imagined to be a huge Glam Rock style single. *Breakdown* was supposed to be the space we blended all those elements into a cohesive whole.

We were always very proud of that album. For me, no matter who criticised it or why, I could always turn around and say *"Fuck you. It's fucking great."*

Ultimately, that's all you can hope to do. When you can say this fucking thing was in our heads and we pulled it out and it turned out just the way we had hoped it would, that's a victory over death. Because death doesn't care; it just wants to drag you off and be done with you.

And one final sidenote; Parrot's drumming is frigging awesome.

SIXTY-SIX

George Street, Sydney, 1978

Her name was Jamie and she drummed with the Idle Idols. I kind of got the feeling that this band was more of an idea than a going concern. It didn't matter. In those days, so many bands were just glorious concepts.

It was a cool name and sometimes that's enough. Even as a notion, I knew greatness when it kicked me in the balls. Besides, with the rest of the band still stuck in New Zealand, there was little chance that my illusions would be shattered. To my mind, the Idle Idols remain the greatest band in human history.

Dressed in an alluring confection of nylon and shredded blue and emerald rags, she looked kind of like a mermaid except she had legs. (But mermaids get legs when they get out of the water, right?) I guess you could say she was more like a siren than a mermaid but that's just giving the game away in advance. I'm telephoning in my plot twists but sometimes the rocks and reefs just don't matter when it comes to the greater scheme of things.

At least now, I've already got you guessing how fatale this femme might be. I used to say that I wanted my life to be like a movie and have all the boring bits edited out. Jamie always claimed her life was better than any movie. She was probably right but she probably had more chilling backstories than me.

I had to come up with a cunning plan to ensure that this would be more than a sighting across a crowded room. I raised my game and busted some moves. I borrowed heavily from the big book of rock guitar poses. I was already wearing a police jacket stolen from the garbage bin outside of Darlinghurst Nick. I was certainly styling and profiling.

I was surprised (and yet vaguely appalled) at how well such posturing went down with the maddened throng. I was also worried about how much fun I was having with these antics. It was not the natural behaviour of the serious revolutionary man I had imagined myself to be. Would the God of Authentic Artistry still let me into Heaven?

My guitar wailed feedback from against the amplifier as I left the stage. The song didn't end until someone got it together to pull the plug but we didn't have a road crew. The final song of the night could go on for a fuck of a long time. The fact was, I could have just left the thing whining away all night so it'd still be set up for the gig the next day.

For me, the guitar hero thing was done and dusted for the night. It was time to find new mountains to scale. Andi and Ross, knew me well enough to spot the course my one-track mind was taking. I had the aura of an accident about to happen. They rolled their eyes and quietly shook their heads. I was about to make an idiot out of myself again and the only questions that remained involved just how I would achieve this idiocy and how stupid it would be.

I had but two words on my lips as a marched through the crowd.

I repeated them to anyone who paused to speak with me.

Roller Disco!

Whether I was working from a platform of genius or madness was open to debate. My mind was not a pacific afternoon lulled by gentle ocean breezes. It was a rat-infested maze of possibility. As far as I can tell, the only real difference between inspiration and insanity is the ability to communicate ideas. I feel I must therefore offer some small words of explanation.

A couple of blocks down George Street, someone had set up a small rink to cash in on a new trend shipped in from the States. Just how big this trend was in the US was anyone's guess. Someone had probably seen something in a movie. You know. One of those low brow things where the kids throw their hands in the air like they just don't care. Something completely unlike any party you have ever been to.

There was that album with Linda Ronstadt on the cover wearing roller skates. Maybe the owners had seen that and finally imagined a use for that bare concrete floor. Perhaps they imagined if they built it, she would come.

This, however, was a time when fads had to start themselves from the bottom without the help of an army of marketing consultants or a herd of focus groups. Importing trends did not impress the predominate cynicism of the time. You could work that out by simply taking a quick look at the Grand. It arose out of kids doing it for themselves. The version of punk being created there may have taken cues from overseas but it lacked the fashion police fascism of our London cousins. Sydney was far too fucking hot for that kind of conceit.

Naturally, skating round in circles to disco music had gone down like a lead balloon in Sydney. It actively defied the cultural imperative that demanded Aussie males gather around the bar and ignore their women lest they be accused of homosexuality. If it hadn't been for the dubious deals involving pills and powders going on in the back room, the place would have closed down months earlier. Far removed from the eyes of the suburban sprawl, the rink was constantly empty but the beat went on and on.

After a few visits, I had felt the public address system dipping a toe towards Blondie and the Stranglers and Elvis Costello. They may only have been exposed to what 2SM considered New Wave but the management had an eye for a developing market.

So, here was my master plan. It was eleven o'clock and the pub would be chucking out. Sheila, the Grand's barmaid, was already giving out steely looks like she had somewhere else to go that didn't involve us. Her real name wasn't Shiela but she wasn't a punk. She was like one of those Sheilas who hung around Bruces. Sheila was a non-ethnic based slur based around normality. A female bogan. But Sheila was our barmaid.

As hard as it is to believe today, just about all pubs chucked out at eleven and the night was over. There was nothing you could do about it. Some pubs tried to get around it by serving "*meals*" to their clientele. This generally meant they were inciting food fights involving stale sausage rolls that would have to be cleaned up the following morning.

The Bondi Lifesaver had a late licence but it was in Bondi and, if you relied on public transport, that might as well have been out the back of Bourke. Besides, as mentioned earlier, the Lifesaver usually offered up the kind of music only your big brother liked.

I had to find a way to talk to this green haired vision. I had to do it quickly. There were no parties on but the disco would be rolling on 'til late. If I could convince a mass grouping to come down the road, I was fairly certain I could use what little charm I possessed in order to convince her to join us. After all, it was a safe family style outing, chaperoned by a leprous mob of scurvy drunkards. What girl could refuse an offer like that?

Besides, skating was fun and, probably thanks to the unbearable boredom of Wollongong, I could actually roller skate well enough not to make a complete idiot out of myself.

I also liked *Roller Derby* from *Channel 10* and often tried to dig through the snow of poor transmission to see what team of baddies threatened the Los Angeles Thunderbirds on any particular week. The baddy teams looked like the same people every week with different costumes. It was professional wrestling on wheels.

I knew how uncool it was. One could not, for example, imagine *Johnny Rotten*, *Iggy Pop* or *Joe Strummer* strapping a pair of skates to their feet. It was an activity that could go pear shaped so very easily. Your average rock star will do anything to avoid going arse over tit.

But fun is fun and between you and me, skating was one of my guilty pleasures. By any professional standard, I was crap but next to the wasted horde of the Grand's clientele, I was a god. I'd been practicing. How else do you suppose I knew about the place?

As cunning schemes went, it was unbelievably ridiculous. Yet, through stubborn force of will, the calling in of favours and a studied maniacal glance borrowed from Manson and Rasputin, I soon had a motley crew moving northwards through the night. Best still, I had convinced Jamie to join us on our wheeled crusade.

Pretty soon, there was a mob of tight jeaned and leather (or pretend leather plastic) jacket clad fools making like Bambi on polished concrete. Everyone was laughing and falling on their arses to the throbbing beats of *Donna Summer* and *Boney M*. Big dumb fun is wasted on the young.

The owner didn't know whether to shit himself or rejoice at the sight of paying customers. You could tell he was weighing off potential drug sales against increased police scrutiny.

SIXTY-SEVEN
London 1985

The album came out to what could at best be called mixed reviews. Sounds gave it five stars. NME was less positive with a review that seemed to revolve entirely about a party we had attended and apparently wreaked untold havoc at. No-one in the band could actually remember attending this party. Maybe it was supposed to be a metaphor but the writer didn't seem that clever. I think, however, we all wanted to turn up at the writer's next event and make her dreams come true.

We had all received some white labels which were mostly handed out for promotional purposes like reviews and radio play. I wanted a proper copy and was told there were about thirty copies at Virgin Records at Tottenham Court Road. By the time I got there, they'd all been sold. They were sold out everywhere. In fact, it would take me twenty-five odd years to secure a copy in Japan of all places.

We set about getting a few gigs together to promote a disc that had essentially sold out and, because of the mysteries of capitalism and the time it took for money to return and finance a second pressing, would vanish out of print.

The big gig was the *Ambulance Station* on Old Kent Road. A week before, *The Jesus and Mary Chain* had had a fairly big turnout. When we played, people were literally hanging out of the rafters. A coach had been hired to bring people down from Scotland.

There were legs dangling off cross beams five metres above the dance floor.

We had said we were going to do two sets. The first set was going to be based around the album. The second set was going to be some of the older material from the *Anarchy Centre* days. Songs like *Paradise*, *Jesus*, *Curse on You*, *Love Under Will*, and *Mummy*. We also thought we'd play some cover versions. It was supposed to be a reward for the audience for putting up with the newer stuff and we knew stuff like *Breakdown* was going to be challenging.

Breakdown, in fact, was met with a deafening silence. We would have had a better reaction if we'd shat in the audience's mouth. We quickly got back in the audience's good graces with *Some Like It Hot* and *Possession* but, I'll tell you, it's easier to deal with rabid abuse than stunned and disapproving silence.

Of course, things didn't go as planned and, sure as shit, some less than happy local resident or publican phoned in a bomb threat and the building had to be emptied. By the time everything got back on track, it was getting late. After we played thirty minutes of the first set, we were told we couldn't play a second set. We played a couple of *Stooges* songs and called it a night.

As we were packing up, Lisa told me that, whilst she'd been off scoring drugs in Brixton, she'd bumped into an old friend of mine. A few days later, we were playing at the Underground in Croydon and there was Jamie.

Oh, oh. Here comes trouble.

SIXTY-EIGHT
Kings Cross, Sydney, 1978

Punks were pretty much at the top of the law and order hit list since the gay community had got organised and started hitting back. There had been fighting in Oxford Street and the police had their collective butts handed to them. Most of the local punks had joined in the fight because we were all fed up of being bullied by the cops.

The anniversary of that battle is celebrated every year as the Sydney Gay and Lesbian Mardi Gras.

Not wanting to admit that they could be beaten up by homosexuals, the cops decided to leave well enough alone and start hunting out new prey. The cops hated us because we looked like criminals but weren't generating enough income from crime to pay them bribes. If we'd have only just played the game and started selling drugs to school kids then we would have been fine. Instead, life became an endless round of not so random searches served with the odd fist to the guts and slap to the face. We were only safe when we were off the streets.

Many days were spent chasing an endless run of parties and playing a particularly fun game called bathroom bingo. This unique game had one rule. You crashed the party, hit the bathroom and downed one of every pill you found in the medicine cabinet. As doctors were far freer with their prescriptions in those days, the chances were good that you would end up off of your face. Alternatively, you could go blind or find yourself growing what appeared to be a third testicle. What the hell. You're only young once. You could also wake up in the women's toilet of the Grand, puking your guts out. And that was fun too.

It was ten minutes before I was supposed to play when I emerged from unconsciousness to find myself collapsed over the bowl. Jamie slapped me about a bit and convinced me to rinse out my mouth. She pointed me towards the stage and splashed cold water on my face. I was quietly touched that anyone could care enough to deal with my shit. My shit was generally just cause for comic relief.

After the gig, she took me back to her house. I was stupid enough to believe she actually wanted me to come up to her room so she could show me this cool portable television she had just bought. Thankfully, she didn't want to watch TV. Unfortunately, she was catching a plane home the next day.

At around three in the morning, a guy came in and told Jamie they had a couple of guys down the road and asked whether she was interested. The money, apparently, was good. She thought it over, jacked the price up a little higher and told me to wait because this wouldn't take more than half an hour.

SIXTY-NINE

New Cross, London, 1986

Back in high school, I had this history teacher called Mister Slatcher. His version of history came complete with a whole mess of right-wing philosophies which the sheep eagerly jotted down in their quests for good grades. True or false didn't matter. Obedience to your mentor was everything. It was a message I repeatedly failed to understand.

Life is so much easier if you will only believe whatever bullshit is served your way.

Like some raggedy old scarecrow, street prophet, skeleton, *Peter Cushing* motherfucker, he would hang from the blackboard and proclaim democracy was doomed. Historically, he reasoned, democracies will always fall into chaos from which will eventually emerge vicious dictatorships because this is what happened in ancient times.

He was probably right but I didn't like his alternative.

Mr Slatcher thought that, rather than battle to maintain a strong democracy by educating the populace, the way to prevent the fall into inevitable fascism was by creating and maintaining a strong benevolent dictatorship in the form of a monarchy. If you didn't have a convenient monarch, you could always use a mythical being that looked like *Hitler* but had the heart of *Charlie Chaplin*.

Mr Slatcher smoked a pipe in class like the ghost of *Neville Chamberlain*. He rained cancer down upon us in thick blue clouds. There was not a single gasp of air to be found that had not passed through his tar filled lungs

A poorly argued criticism of his rabid ideology would earn you a C on the grounds that you were not paying attention to his version of history. A well-argued attack would earn you an F on the grounds that you were a vile, evil servant of Satan, *Stalin* and anarchy. Suggesting that this may have, in itself, demonstrated the injustice inherent in any form of dictatorship would earn you little besides the blank stares of your fellow students.

Our beloved Gruppenführer would have perfectly understood this as nascent socialism; an argument that could pretty much earn you an expulsion from his classroom on the spot. Fortunately, although corporate punishment was acceptable and, indeed, encouraged, capital punishment was not legal in school. Mr Slatcher had access to the cane.

The reason I bring up Herr Slatcher is that I am struck now by one of the more arcane beliefs he had imparted to us. To him, the universe was like a big machine. The planets spun like tiny cogs in a giant clock. In a version of physics ultimately discredited by acceptance of *Einstein*'s description of the time space continuum, everything was perfectly made and perfectly planned. This was God's universe and the job of science was to reveal these wonders. God was perfect and his perfect clockwork Universe was certain evidence of his existence. Who else could keep the clock wound?

Einstein is also alleged to have said that, had he known that the horrors of the atom bomb would be made possible by his theories, he would have rather been a watchmaker. And why not? Watches are a simple mechanism based on simple physics and simple rules. There are no rogue comets or black holes and the cold death of entropy is solved by the winding of a spring. There are no surprises. No chaos. No life cluttering up the gears with its own selfish and war-like interests.

If God had made such a universe, he would have placed it in a vacuum jar and kept its beauty sterile. Because if God was omnipotent, he'd know what kind of a mess that life would make of the place. He'd know about the scum that forms around the edges of a tank. If we were made in his image, he'd also know something of our pains and heartaches and would spare us the worst of them. Those who were made in his image are the very worst of men.

When I remember Mr Slatcher holding court over his ticking clock universe, part of me is disgusted by how little life had touched him; how wars, starvation and suffering were occurrences to be recorded. And part of me is more jealous than I can bear to describe. Ignorance is a bliss I often strive for but reality just keeps getting in the way.

At least an oyster makes pearls of its suffering. We merely abide.

Jamie was in a state of distress. She had her own version of the clockwork universe going on; a clock that needed winding. The cocktail of opiates, tranquillisers, amphetamines and barbiturates had been administered according to her own special recipe. She needed to be oblivious to their ashtray breath and cruel thrusts. Some guys just don't seem to be able to come unless they're hurting you.

The kind of guy who never looked her in the eye because he was too busy exploring the valley between her tits. Basically, the kind of guy who sought her out on the city streets. The guys with sweaty palms and dirty money.

And the late-night streets seemed to attract a particular kind of clientele. Gamblers from Mayfair and a certain low class of celebrity scum. Politicians, lesser ranked royalty and the well-heeled wowsers with their old school ties.

I'd heard enough stories to make my skin crawl off my bones.

There had been many times she had appeared at my door in the early hours. Beaten, bruised; I patched her up or took her somewhere that would.

Getting that money was a necessity. She just didn't want too much of her higher brain functions asking the obvious fucking question: "*What the fuck are you doing to yourself?*" And, quite frankly, who the fuck could blame her. Being oblivious is one thing but then there's the razor thin line between being oblivious and oblivion.

Her clock was running out. The countdown was in place. Tick. Tock. Little chemical time bombs were dissolving in her stomach.

Tiny particles found their way through intestines into the bloodstream. Livers and kidneys winced at the thought of another hard day's cleaning and purging (ultimately to no avail). Greedy little receptor cells clawed eagerly at the red current.

Stop my pain. Stop my pain. Tick. Tock. Tick fucking tock.

The whole system had to be maintained. One small break in the chain would bring the whole fucker down around her ears. Withdrawal? Don't fucking go there. Heroin is such a holy drug. You got that whole mind body schism thing going on so well that the Pope should put your name down for sainthood. Sex means nothing. Christ, you don't even have to shit. On top of that, you kind of look like Jesus after the Romans had kicked the living crap out of him and that was on your good days.

"Please come with me."

Well, that was the last thing I would ever want to do. This was not a world I wanted to play a part in.

"I can't. I'm working tomorrow."

It was three in the morning and I started at nine thirty. God fucking damn.

"Please."

She and I both knew I would go with her. She knew I'd fold.

And so, the taxi was called. I resigned myself to staring out at the world outside. There's nothing to see South of the River. You could be in any poxy city in the Western World until you hit the Vauxhall Bridge. Sure, there are pockets of interest but these are dispersed between the endless nothingness of the orange street lights and council estates.

Ah. But once you cross the Thames. Magic.

The city is special when the pubs have long chucked out their last drunks and the nine to fivers have scurried off into slumber. The electric lighting does not sleep in the night even though the witnesses have fled. The coloured bulbs of shop displays keep dancing and the advertising slogans suddenly take on a deep intimacy.

When the streets are full, the signs are no different from the street preachers and the lunatics. They scream loudly but are heard by no-one. At night you are alone with them and they whisper seductively of better lives.

The big brand names come out to play. The dreams of sleeping bankers made real. I've heard it said that artists and witches use the night because they draw their powers from the unconscious minds of honest folk. When I first heard that, part of me wanted to believe it because it sounded cool. My rational side, however, dismissed the notion.

Then I entered the underworld of the city.

Sirens called from billboards, promising all would be well if you owned an American Express card. The jagged rocks at their feet remained concealed by smiles and visible cleavage. Bus shelters that housed sleeping derelicts displayed the legends of elixirs and potions; fountains of youth. Promises wrapped in the fairy glamour of neon.

And yes, I knew it was glamour. Glamour in its original sense. The meaning that time forgot. It did not bother me that it was lies. Reality was waiting at journey's end. The Eastern sky reddened to the rising sun.

I cosied up to illusion where it is safer.

SEVENTY

George Street, Sydney 1978

In the morning, a taxi rolled up and she was gone. It had not been the grand romance I had envisioned. But we find people as we move through life, we make connections and those connections are the things that make our lives real. Like tiny quantum particles, we become entangled and, no matter how far we travel we are still bound; their words and ideas coming back with memory. For good or ill, those words still shape us.

I often consider how much those bonds hold especially as so many pass. Are we all just a collection of our ghosts and our traumas? We are exceptionally linked by our worst moments.

Sydney suddenly felt a whole lot duller. I spent the day at the movies, a return to the refuge of my youth. I started early on George Street. When one session ended, I sought out another. George Street was one long parade of cinemas then and I wasn't being fussy. I was chasing a feeling.

I watched *Linda Blair* rotate her head and *John Belushi* impersonate a pimple to much the same end. In an even poorer decision, I watched *Clint Eastwood* buddy up with a fucking orang-outang. It did little to improve my mood.

Then it was back to the Grand to play the whole damn set again.

I suppose I was having a moment. I was probably depressed. The streets were all haunted by spirits of better times and the bands all started to sound the same. My world was being swallowed by third generation clichés. Everyone had started stabbing everyone's back over who was the best when we all just simply were there together. Instead of rehearsing and writing some better songs, the world increasingly aimed at a bar set to our lowest expectations. Maybe, they always had been and I'd just been too self-absorbed to notice.

Maybe the new was getting old. It was time to make a change.

More by accident than design, I had given up on living anywhere and only now do I realise how broken I had become. When I needed to sleep, I searched out couches and balconies and parks. I was pushing at chaos and looking for a plan, something to reignite the fire. I needed a dream. And then, at a party (and I've already gone on record to describe how much I dislike parties), I walked out the door saying *"Fuck this. I'm going to London."*

SEVENTY-ONE
London, 1986

By this stage, Lisa and Ralph seemed to have developed habits of an epic proportion. They told me they had met John from the *Only Ones* at a doctor's surgery in Ladbroke Grove. You can imagine the practice's speciality. This was around the time *Peter Perrett* was getting arrested in car park fights in America.

The idea was we would all go on tour together with them to America but I knew we didn't have any money and no promoter or record company would touch us even with rubber gloves and a hazmat suit. The whole thing sounded like drug induced bullshit but they were treating it like it was all arranged and a done deal.

I was sick to death of being the grown up. I just walked. If it had happened, it would have been a death trip with a quick stop off at Rikers Island along the way. I was burnt out and wanted to indulge in some bad behaviour of my own. I was rather keen on the idea of sleeping for a thousand years by whatever means necessary.

I played one more gig with Lisa at the *Half Moon* in Herne Hill. That was to an audience of exactly no-one. A headline gig in an empty room, we were well rehearsed and playing at the top of our game. The last gig we'd played in that neighbourhood was the *Brixton Ace* and that was fairly close to a capacity of 2,000. Whatever it was we were selling now, it was pretty clear nobody was buying.

A week might be a long time in politics but the music business can break you in half the time.

Sometimes your London privileges just run out. London only wants you under very specific circumstances. Many people are under the illusion that talent is one of these in demand virtues but London doesn't want your talent. In London, every fucker and his pet dog has a talent.

The world was turning on its axis once again. Night had not only come down. The stars in the sky had also begun to fall. One single lonely death after another.

Smack was being challenged by crack as the street drug of choice. The world was turning mean. Say what you will about junkies but, if they can't get a fix, they writhe around and sweat but they're pretty much locked to their toilet for three days. A crackhead just gets crankier. Suddenly, I was getting mugged every time I went to the corner store.

Once they discovered I had Ventolin inhalers, they just wanted them. I didn't even know why. Maybe they used Ventolin to try to get more crack in their lungs.

Friends suddenly started showing me their newly acquired guns. Ammunition seemed their major concern but they insisted they could get me a pistol complete with a couple of rounds for a hundred quid. Maybe one fifty tops. I was less than interested in making this kind of purchase but, then again, I wasn't doing crack.

Walking the streets of Nunhead late one night, I was confronted by an albino fox. It stood in front of me, blocking my path. It stared me in the eye and I almost expected it to speak. I read this as omen.

London expects you to be young or rich. If you're young it wants to fuck you and fuck you up bad. If you're rich, it expects you to pay for all your fucks. My dancing days were clearly over. It was time to fuck off and give some other poor deluded bastard a go.

SEVENTY-TWO
London, 1979

Johnny Dole and the Scabs had pretty much learnt how to be a functional rock and roll band playing a Stones influenced punk style. They had decided to try their luck in London. Strategically changing their name to the *Crooked Hearts*, they needed a bass player. I told them that I could do that so at least there was a door I could darken at the other end of the flight.

The plane had landed in Singapore on the way over. A stewardess had advised me not to leave the plane as I might not meet with the expectations of the local authorities. I was quite used to not meeting up to the expectations of locals and authorities.

My mother had lived in Marylebone and worked in service to the more affluent surrounding suburbs. I found myself in her old stomping ground but felt no connection to these roots. Wealth still butted against poverty and, whilst some streets were filled with the posh branded Paris, Milan, New York vibe, Marylebone High Street still looked as though it was unsure the war was over.

I began to suspect the *Crooked Hearts* were a doomed enterprise. We practiced daily in a single shared room sans amps and drum kit. We went out looking for a squat and potential gigs. We knew no-one and had no contacts. Worst still, we had no money. We would go to the pub and imagine drowning our sorrows. At best, we could only afford to give them a quick dip.

I had bought a one-way ticket. Bridges were for burning.

Not recognizing disinterest as our biggest foe, John conjured the idea that coming from Australia would make us hated. He perpetually dreamed of what he would say at gigs to win over the imagined crowds. He practiced his banter like we practiced our instruments. He was a would-be magician trying to will a world into existence but existence was having none of it. The rent was about to fall due.

On the last night, long after sunset, John went out. I can't say I believe in auras but he was surrounded by an air of evil and blackness I have only seen surround the most psychotic. It was as if there was a devil upon his shoulder born of frustration and despair.

When he returned several hours later, he was clearly shaken. He said he'd killed someone with a brick, a dosser in an alley. His story was largely met with disbelief and I knew he could be somewhat unreliable with the truth. The conversation in the room revolved around how that could not possibly be true. There was, for instance, no blood to even hint of the legitimacy of the tale.

You'd think there would be blood, right? Huge pools of out damn spot Macbeth hand wringing guilt. The kind of evidence that you could hide from neither God nor man.

His girlfriend was from France and I knew he was looking for a way to walk away from this London debacle without admitting failure. But the lie was too big for purpose.

I was probably the only person convinced he was telling the truth. There was something in his eyes, a wild haunted stare. Even if it had been a lie or only an exaggeration of a lesser incident, who the fuck makes shit like that up?

Whilst the band would be departing in the morning towards the Continent, I made it abundantly clear I would not be joining them. I may have been nuts but I wasn't fucking nuts. Nobody suggested we should all stick together. No-one sought to dissuade me. Maybe it, was all an elaborate ruse to kick me to the kerb. Maybe, I really hoped it was.

Had a crime been committed? Where was it committed? What was the real name of this Johnny Dole? Where did he go? How the fuck would I know?

Who the fuck knows anyone or anything?

So, there I was, sitting in Hyde Park, skint homeless and pretty much in shock. The sun was gone and night had won. I broke down and cried for a couple of minutes before getting up and deciding to survive. Surely, it could only get better.

AFTERWORD

"Nothing is True. Everything is permitted."

Friedrich Nietzsche

Mick Lugworm of the *Turdburglars* used to print out tiny stickers and leave them on phone boxes, backs of bus seats and basically any nailed down hard surface. Others followed suit. Amongst the slogans displayed, this one by Nietzsche was prominent.

As Tony D recently told me *"Alistair produced those ones. Luggy started the idea with anarcho type slogans and I did some Crowley type ones. Alistair did his one using black ink on gold background. He brought it in from Robert Anton Wlson's Illuminatus Trilogy.*

It was also used by Burroughs in his books Naked Lunch, Nova Express and The Ticket That Exploded, his cut-up novels. The phrase is attributed by Burroughs (perhaps apocryphally) as the last words of Hassan ibn Sabbah, aka "The Old Man of the Mountain," the legendary founder of a guerilla group called the hashashins (supposedly the origin of the word "assassin," (so-called because they allegedly used hashish before they went into battle).

Nietzsche's intended meaning of that expression is that there is no absolute moral force and therefore we should not be guided by a moral force. Whilst this book appears as a story about punks and music, a memoir of sorts, I think it is mostly about that quote.

This certainly is a story where those words are taken out for a ride. They are driven as if they were stolen. People often seem to live in very different worlds despite receiving identical inputs from their surroundings. The chemistry of our body betrays us even before we start messing with that chemistry. I have probably made a fairly good case for the "*nothing is true*" part of the equation.

So, I suppose the question I have to ask is "*should everything be permitted?*"

Surely, we want no part of Gods or Masters but how do we come to terms with each other? If everything is permitted, nobody else matters.

That is why I like to say "*Love is the Law*".

I say this because we shouldn't all be wandering around trying to be *the superman*. We are a social animal and we work best when we work together. We have plenty of differences but we have far more in common.

I owe this book to a lot of people. I owe it to *Murray Engleheart* (author of *Radio Birdman: Retaliate First*, *AC/DC: Maximum Rock and Roll* and *Blood, Sweat and Beers*). He told me to write more and so I did. Some years earlier, *Robert Brokenmouth* tried to bully me in the same direction and I have tried to incorporate some of his suggestions but, sorry *Robert*, this is about as close as my brain gets to a linear structure.

I especially owe this book to Tara Anderson who forgives me my dives into hyperfocus and gently reminds me to be human and tells me when I'm supposed to be doing other things like eating or taking the dog out for a walk.

I owe it to *Tony Drayton* and *Alistair Livingstone* who, through fanzines like *Ripped and Torn*, *Kill Your Pet Puppy* and the *Encyclopedia of Ecstasy* legitimised a style of writing that peppered within itself obscure quotes from the edges of popular culture. For me, it has become a very dynamic tool where, like a picture, you can paint a thousand words with a single borrowed song lyric.

Then, there are a lot of people who are now dead but who certainly played a large part in the narrative you have read. This includes a frightening number of musicians I have played with over the years. I considered writing a list but became frightened of the likelihood I would miss out a name. Additionally, it is a list that grows all the time. Regrettably, each amendment would provide scope for more amendments.

Many of us did not expect to grow old. I do, however, hope some of these stories invoke memories and we can all keep some of those times alive. You may have been there and you may remember these stories differently. You may wonder why you didn't rate a mention. There maybe the chance you were actually good and kind to me and that didn't play well with this narrative.

Finally, I argue that nothing is true and everything is true. I argue everything is permitted but only if done with love and respect. I thank you for reading and hope you leave entertained or, at the very least, horrified. This was, however, a book about a dark time and I see dark times coming again.

As you read through this book, I'm sure you have seen that some victories for progress have occurred. We have also seen some of those victories snatched back. Let us be united in hope.

Bob Short April 2025

About the Author

Bob Short was born in Dagenham, Essex and now lives in Sydney, Australia. He claims to have seen the yellow lights go down the Mississippi but that might be apocryphal. He is a musician, song writer, writer, artist and filmmaker. Largely operating deep beneath the mainstream, his has worked on albums like Blood and Roses' *"Enough is Never Enough"*, The Light Brigade's *"Going Underground"* and his solo album *"Et Mourir de Plaisir"*. His books include *"Trash Can"*, *"Filth"* and the comic *"Red, White and Blue"*. He continues to work on numerous projects considering each completed work a small victory over death.

Anarcho-Punk:
Music and Resistance
in London 1977-1988

Anarcho-Punk: Music and Resistance in London 1977-1988 by David Insurrection is the distillation of three years work. It's the story of an oft overlooked scene. Anarcho-punk in the 1980s truly rocked the boat. Much more than music it set out to change the world and in a not insignificant way did just that. It inspired a generation of activists, artists and musicians to take up the fight for a better fairer world. They tore down the walls. The Sex Pistols may have opened the door but the Crass punks charged through it. This is their story. As we return to the embattled 1970s and 1980s David takes us on a journey where we visit some of the scene's most significant locations and hot spots, to places where change mattered and the spirit of revolt burned brightest.

Available now at
www.earthislandbooks.com

"The U.K. Subs are the soundtrack for so many of us. Charlie's voice is one of a kind. He's our voice of the voiceless. He's our elder statesman. He's our King of Punk. Long live the king."
Lars Frederiksen (Rancid)

AN ANARCHY OF DEMONS

CHARLIE HARPER

Available now in paperback, hardback and ebook at
www.earthislandbooks.com

https://facebook.com/UK
https://uksubstimeandma

USED

ARTCORE FANZINE PRESENTS

NEFARIOUS

THE EVOLUTION AND ART OF THE PUNK ROCK, POST-PUNK, NEW WAVE,

33RPM   NA001

HARDCORE PUNK AND ALTERNATIVE ROCK COMPILATION RECORD

ARTISTS

1976 - 1989

WELLY ARTCORE

EARTH ISLAND BOOKS

WWW.EARTHISLANDBOOKS.COM   WWW.ARTCOREFANZINE.CO.UK

Long before online streaming and even TV music videos, that were beyond the reach of many new bands outside of a lucky spin on the radio, the compilation became the most effective way to access, and be accessed by, the eager new ears and inquisitive minds of the then new punk generation. 'Nefarious Artists' is a field study of over 500 punk rock, post-punk, new wave, hardcore punk, and alternative rock compilations from their beginnings in 1976 as major label samplers and live showcases of the 'new wave'

www.ingramcontent.com/pod-product-compliance
Ingram Content Group UK Ltd.
Pitfield, Milton Keynes, MK11 3LW, UK
UKHW020103030925
462464UK00008B/21